370

# THE NEW BANKER
## DEVELOPING LEADERSHIP
## IN A DYNAMIC ERA

# THE NEW BANKER
## DEVELOPING LEADERSHIP
## IN A DYNAMIC ERA

*James H. Donnelly, Jr.*
*Steven J. Skinner*

**Dow Jones-Irwin**
Homewood, Illinois 60430

Sponsoring editor: Jim Childs
Project editor: Waivah Clement
Production manager: Irene H. Sotiroff
Cover designer: Sam Concialdi
Compositor: Eastern Graphics Typographers
Typeface: 11/13 Century Schoolbook
Printer: R. R. Donnelley & Sons Company

**Library of Congress Cataloging-in-Publication Data**

Donnelly, James H., Jr.
  The new banker : developing leadership in a dynamic era / James H.
Donnelly, Jr., and Steven J. Skinner.
    p.    cm.
  Includes index.
  ISBN 1-55623-177-6
  1. Bank management.  2. Executive ability.  I. Skinner, Steven J.
II. Title.
HG1615.D66  1989                                          89–32052
332.1'068—dc20                                               CIP

*Printed in the United States of America*

1 2 3 4 5 6 7 8 9 0 DO 6 5 4 3 2 1 0 9

*To:*
*Bob and Rosejane Smith (M&D)*
*Connie Donnelly and Helene Donnelly*
*Moira, Aaron, and Carrie Skinner*
*John and Dorothy Skinner*

# PREFACE

In the mid-1970s, one of us was having dinner with two friends. One was a bank CEO, the other an executive with a high-tech manufacturing firm. The banker mentioned that he was leaving town later in the week to attend an industry leadership conference. The executive looked puzzled, not knowing that such meetings focused on lobbying strategies and not on developing management and leadership skills. Finally, he chuckled and said, "Leadership? There can be no such thing as leadership in the banking industry. What will you do at this meeting?"

While the executive's comment may or may not have had some validity in 1975, it certainly would have none today. In fact, this book will argue that management and leadership skills have become critical in banking since deregulation. And they are needed in *all* managerial jobs.

*The New Banker* is based on over five years of systematic field research, which included interviews with several hundred bank officers, interviews or survey responses from more than 300 CEOs, as well as discussions with the nation's leading banking educators, association executives, consultants, and members of the press. It became clear to us that most if not all banks are far more deficient in management skills than they are in banking skills. Furthermore, the challenge to banking in the 1990s will not be retraining workers, but retraining managers, especially middle managers.

Our goal was to write a book that can be immediately useful to those bankers who also manage or aspire to manage people, parts of banking organizations, or entire organizations. *The*

*New Banker* has two specific purposes: (1) to help bankers create a management and leadership capacity in their organization, and (2) to help bankers in their own career and professional development as they seek to develop their own managerial and leadership capabilities.

The core of our book focuses on the three managerial concerns that dominated the thinking of the senior bankers to whom we spoke:

1. Developing an organization where everyone does their best work. We term this people challenge a *performance culture*.
2. Managing change, including identifying when change is needed, and implementing and overcoming resistance to change.
3. Developing a responsive organization structure. We found many banks trying to use yesterday's organization structure to get them to tomorrow.

Not only are these critical managerial challenges but, in our opinion, they constitute the underlying causes of many other problems that bank managers face daily.

We conclude our book with a chapter that focuses on the career and professional development of the new banker, and we identify the specific challenges facing the banker, the bank, and the industry.

We owe the Prochnow Educational Foundation of Madison, Wisconsin, a debt of gratitude for providing the support for the final phase of the field research on which the book is based. As a consequence of the Foundation's support, *The New Banker* has a firmer foundation in research.

We must also single out for special thanks the CEOs and senior bankers who participated in our interviews and the CEOs who participated in our survey. Our book would not have been possible without their assistance.

This book would also not have been possible without our many banker friends who repeatedly fueled our guilt feelings for taking a Saturday afternoon off by continually asking "When is your book going to be finished?"

Finally, our sponsoring editor, Jim Childs of Dow Jones-Irwin, deserves special recognition. His suggestions have made this a better book for the reader. There is nothing like working with professionals, and Jim Childs is a pro in every respect.

So, for bankers who manage or aspire to manage, this book's for you. We want to inform but we also want to inspire you to implement, because reading and doing nothing will mean we have all wasted our time.

*James H. Donnelly, Jr.*
*Steven J. Skinner*

# ACKNOWLEDGMENTS

In the twenty years I have spent as an academic involved in the banking industry as a teacher, writer, and consultant I have learned a great deal from hundreds of bankers. There are several banker friends and colleagues who have made tremendous contributions to my professional development over the years. This book provides me with the opportunity to acknowledge this intellectual debt.

Each one is or has been a banker. But they are also teachers. I have worked with them at industry schools, sat in their classes, listened to them lecture, and debated and discussed issues with them. I have consulted with some of them. A few of them I rarely see anymore. I owe a great intellectual debt to each of them because I not only have learned from them, but they also provided a great deal of intellectual inspiration to a then young, and now not-so-young academic. Thank you,

**Martin J. Allen**
*Senior Vice President*
Old Kent Financial Corp.
Grand Rapids, Mich.

**Joseph C. Cantwell**
*Director of Planning*
Elser and Aucone Inc.
New York, N.Y.

**Charles F. Haywood**
*Professor of Finance*
University of Kentucky
Lexington, Ky.

**Charles H. McCabe**
*Executive Vice President*
Manufacturers Hanover Trust Co.
New York, N.Y.

**Warner Dalhouse**
*President and CEO*
Dominion Bancshares Corp.
Roanoke, Va.

**William Fackler**
*Executive Vice President*
Barnett Banks of Florida
Jacksonville, Fla.

**John Fisher**
*Senior Vice President*
Bank One Corporation
Columbus, Ohio

**N. W. Pope**
*Senior Vice President*
Valley National Bank
Phoenix, Ariz.

**Richard Rosenberg**
*Vice Chairman*
Bank of America Corporation
San Francisco, Calif.

**Kent D. Stickler**
*President*
Stickler Learning
Clearwater, Fla.

**Jim Donnelly**

# CONTENTS

# PART 1

# THE LEADERSHIP CHALLENGE

Leadership is action, not position.
*Donald H. McGammon*

# CHAPTER 1

---

# BANKERS, MANAGERS, AND LEADERS

---

*No one expects bank CEOs to be able to walk on water, but it's not unreasonable to expect them to show leadership and capability whatever way the weather blows.*

Robert L. Clark

This is a book for bankers, but it is not a book about banking. The basic premise is that, as deregulation progresses, management and managerial issues are becoming critical in the banking industry. Thus, this book focuses on "managing the bank," not on lending, operations, trust, or investments. We wrote it for bankers who must also manage.

More important, this book is for a new kind of banker. The bankers are both young and old, and they work in divisions of large bank-holding companies, community banks, and branch offices. However, *their common characteristic is that they manage differently from other bankers and achieve different results.* In the process, they are transforming entire banks, divisions of banks, and branch offices into effective high-performance cultures capable of surviving and growing in an intensely competitive deregulated marketplace. We know because we have talked with many of them over the last five years, and they helped us write this book.

"New bankers" are technically competent bankers *and* effective managers/leaders. They get results because they inspire and motivate others toward the achievement of a common vision and because they realize the importance of good manage-

ment. Their effectiveness isn't magical or beyond the reach of
most of us. They rely on specific practices to achieve their results, and they have seized their responsibility to manage and
lead.


## BACKGROUND

This book began informally as a result of interacting with students and faculty at the industry's leading banking schools. For
20 years we have been on the faculty at many of these schools.
Through class discussions, informal seminars, and debates in
faculty lounges and local pubs, we gained great insight into the
most important problems and current concerns of bank officers.

### Management Becomes a Topic of Discussion

Over the past several years we detected a shift in the focus of
student discussions. The major concerns, problems, and gripes
dwell less and less on "banking" and more and more on "managing." Accounts of successes, triumphs, and victories point to
management as a root cause. Furthermore, what succeeded in
one bank and not another was, after lengthy analysis and discussion, often traced to managerial behavior.

---

What is holding back many banks has little to do with banking
capability and everything to do with managing capability.

---

We also noticed in our consulting assignments that managerial issues were at the center of many successes and problems, although our clients often did not realize it. Casual
conversations, one-on-one dinners, and rides to the airport re-
vealed that management-related factors such as the inability to
manage change, the organization structure of the bank, or the
climate in the bank often made the difference between success
and failure in otherwise similar circumstances.

It seemed to us that if management of a bank was changing because of deregulation, then the knowledge and skills needed by a manager in a bank would also change. Our goal became writing a book that can be immediately useful to bankers who are also managers.

Throughout the mid-1980s our research became more formal and focused specifically on the problems of managing the bank. Our discussions and interviews with students and faculty at banking schools also became more specific. Participating in national conventions, exchange groups, and state association meetings always included formal and informal interviews and discussions. We learned much from our discussions, interviews, and interactions with some of the nation's most respected bank officers, bank academics, national and state association executives, banking school directors, and members of the banking press whom we have been fortunate to count among our friends. Finally, our consulting assignments were invaluable in sharpening both our thinking and our research efforts. By 1985, we were more convinced than ever that what is holding back many banks has little to do with banking capability and everything to do with managing capability.

## Interest by the Industry

In 1985 and 1986 two major industry reports were published which identified the factors that will be crucial for the success of banking in the years ahead.[1] Each report identified quality of management as the most important single factor that will separate high- and low-performing banks in the future. But neither report identified the meaning of "quality management." Both reports stressed that management behavior in competitive industries differed from that in regulated industries, but neither specified these differences.

For years we had heard the best and the brightest in the industry struggle with the same issue: What is effective management in the banking industry? Many bankers told us, "We need more training in management, not more training in banking." Instinctively, they recognized deregulation changed management into a key success factor in banking. To be sure, a bank can fail because of poor quality loans, economic decline, or any of the usual causes, but poor quality in management must now be added to the list.

## MANAGEMENT BECOMES A SUCCESS FACTOR IN BANKING

The need for greater managerial and leadership skills in banking is the direct result of two factors: (1) the increased competition caused by deregulation, and (2) a previous environment that required good administrative skills, but not necessarily management and leadership skills.

### Increased Competition

Today, most banks are caught somewhere between the clearly defined world of commercial banking and the less certain and still evolving financial services business. The competition is no longer a similar and familiar financial institution down the street. Today the competition includes Sears, Beneficial Finance, AARP, Merrill Lynch, Citicorp, GE, American Express, and many others. Tomorrow, the competition could be 7-Eleven, or Ford or IBM, or even more American banks in the hands of foreign owners.

Yesterday, banks and thrifts competed primarily against each other, and friend and foe alike enjoyed some form of marketplace protection and product line exclusives. In fact, banking held a preeminent position because of its checking account monopoly, its trust business monopoly, and its dominant role in the credit card arena, not to mention the fact that banks alone among depository institutions could engage in commercial lending. Yesterday, banks were the only full-service game in town. Many banks practically owned their markets for years. But that was yesterday.

The increased competitive intensity has changed not only the industry, but the jobs of those who manage in the industry as well. Today's bankers are being asked to develop new strategy, to segment markets, and to develop new products and delivery systems as technology ever widens customer service possibilities. They are being asked to take risks, to innovate, and to change or face the prospect of selling the bank. In short, they must figure out the right things to do for their bank or part of the bank. Then they must develop and sustain an organization capable of implementing the strategy. Developing and implementing new strategy will usually involve convincing others to change and to develop new skills that were not mandatory in the competitive calm of times past. Survival in this dynamic environment hinges on effective management and leadership.

## Management by Administration

Prior to deregulation, management selection decisions ran little risk of failure because most individuals in the industry possessed the knowledge and skills needed to be an effective bank manager. Skill in banking and administration, not management, was the primary basis for selecting bank managers.

---

Effective bank managers make a clear distinction between *banking* and *managing the bank*.

---

In regulated times, a bank could perform very well as long as it had people in management positions with sound banking skills and some administrative capability. By administration, we mean the ability to carry out the activities required by the bank's rules, policies, and procedures. The major strategy of most banks before deregulation was internally focused, maintaining tight controls over internal processes and efficient processing of internal information. Management and leadership, if required at all, were necessary only at the top.

Although banking skills and administrative capability are still critical in banking, banks today require effective management and leadership throughout the organization. Very simply, they need more people who can help them deal effectively with the new environment.

Bank managers at all levels are now being asked on a regular basis to take on more—and new—responsibilities. They are also expected to be catalysts, prompting other people to change, to perform at higher levels, and to put forth the extra effort needed to implement the new tasks. In these circumstances, good banking skills and administrative capability no longer suffice for achieving high levels of bank performance.

Managing in today's bank, therefore, means meeting the leadership challenges brought on by deregulation—improving employee performance, developing market-driven products, developing a responsive and flexible organization structure, increasing productivity, improving service quality, and developing a sales culture, to name just a few. It means producing change and managing the effects of change.

Effective management and leadership was not a critical success factor in banking in the past, but it has now become one. Figure 1–1 illustrates the challenge of managing the bank in an era of transition.

## MOVING INTO THE FIELD

In 1986, after three years of interviewing and speaking with hundreds of bankers and banking educators from all over the nation, it was time to test our ideas in the field. We wanted to determine the critical managerial challenges facing bank managers *today*, because they must meet these challenges head on in order to lead their banks, divisions, departments, or branches through the current era of transition.

The final portion of the research was completed in 1988. It involved two phases: (1) personal interviews with groups of 8 to 12 bank chief executive officers (CEOs) in each of six states and interviews with more than 100 senior bank officers and CEOs from across the country, and (2) mail survey responses from a national sample of CEOs.

**FIGURE 1–1**
**The Changing Job of Management in Banking since Deregulation**

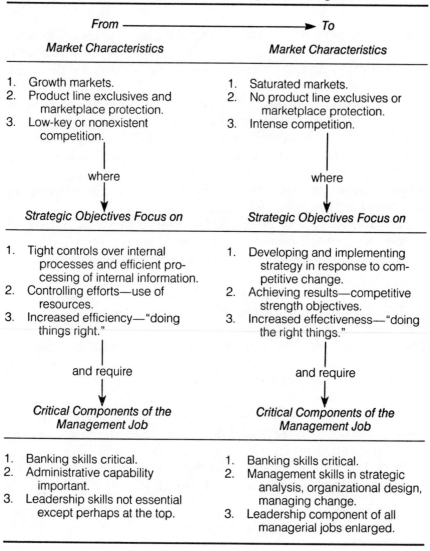

From ⟶ To

*Market Characteristics*  |  *Market Characteristics*

| | |
|---|---|
| 1. Growth markets. | 1. Saturated markets. |
| 2. Product line exclusives and marketplace protection. | 2. No product line exclusives or marketplace protection. |
| 3. Low-key or nonexistent competition. | 3. Intense competition. |

where  |  where

*Strategic Objectives Focus on*  |  *Strategic Objectives Focus on*

| | |
|---|---|
| 1. Tight controls over internal processes and efficient processing of internal information. | 1. Developing and implementing strategy in response to competitive change. |
| 2. Controlling efforts—use of resources. | 2. Achieving results—competitive strength objectives. |
| 3. Increased efficiency—"doing things right." | 3. Increased effectiveness—"doing the right things." |

and require  |  and require

*Critical Components of the Management Job*  |  *Critical Components of the Management Job*

| | |
|---|---|
| 1. Banking skills critical. | 1. Banking skills critical. |
| 2. Administrative capability important. | 2. Management skills in strategic analysis, organizational design, managing change. |
| 3. Leadership skills not essential except perhaps at the top. | 3. Leadership component of all managerial jobs enlarged. |

## LESSONS FROM THE FIELD

Bank managers are remarkably consistent in their opinions about the managerial challenges they face. *The New Banker* is a compilation and synthesis of the ideas shared by the bank managers we interviewed.

Obviously, a banker's approach to the challenges of management will reflect the circumstances of his or her situation. The banker's personality, the nature of the employees, and the demands of the moment will all combine to specify what an individual manager must and can do. But we found a great consistency about the most important managerial challenges they face and how they are facing them.

To introduce *The New Banker,* we outline five important lessons we learned from the individuals we interviewed. These lessons set the stage for the remainder of the book.

### 1. The Components of the Managerial Job in Banking Have Changed

The best bank managers are not only skilled bankers, they are also skilled managers. They know that through leadership they can influence the direction of their bank or part of the bank, and that leadership requires demonstrating competence in managing as well as in banking. In fact, they make a clear distinction between banking and managing the bank. They realize that the managerial job requires more than administration and more than giving instructions and monitoring performance. In this respect they believe, as one CEO said:

> Banks are overadministered and underled. There are too many people in management and leadership roles behaving like civil servants.

The best bank managers believe the leadership component of the managerial job is now the critical component. They also know that bureaucratic managers can be dangerous in an intensely competitive environment. The new banker is clearly a banker, but also a manager and a leader.

## 2. Banks Now Require Good Leadership at Virtually All Levels of the Organization

The best bank managers have made the transition from "I, the manager" to "we, the management." They understand that hierarchical/bureaucratic management with secrecy at the top chokes the creativity and erodes the competitiveness a deregulated environment demands. When no one can make a decision without going through numerous channels and managers spend most of their time protecting their own turfs, little is accomplished. As one CEO put it:

> We must fill positions with managers, not specialists who are successful in a technical area and are rewarded with a management position.

Clearly, the leadership component is expanding in all managerial jobs in banking. Leadership can no longer be the exclusive domain of the CEO.

## 3. Bankers Face Three Critical Management Challenges

Certainly there are others, but three broad areas of concern appear to dominate the thinking of the senior bankers to whom we spoke. And in our opinion the three constitute the underlying causes of many of the problems bank managers deal with daily.

*Developing Performance Cultures.* Bankers from coast to coast voice the necessity and difficulty of getting the best efforts of their people. They use phrases like "peak performance," "going the extra mile," "teamwork," "team building," and "committed employees" to describe their need. Some expressed the need in other quite frank ways:

> We can no longer manage in such a way that a person's biggest weakness determines where he ends up in the bank.

> Telling employees *what* to do is not enough. Today they must also know *why* they do what they do.

We use the term *performance culture* to summarize these concerns. A bank will have a performance culture when every-

one in the bank does their best work. In these banks, management views one of its major responsibilities as providing the
conditions which enable employees to do their best work.

*Managing Change.* Talking about change is becoming
tiresome for most bankers. What they want is the wherewithal
to manage change—to actually bring about needed change
without negatively impacting the bank, "So that the cure doesn't
kill the patient," as one banker said. Bankers express this challenge in a variety of ways. Some state it as the need to "advocate change in my bank" or as "challenging the status quo."
Others want to "encourage innovation" and "overcome resistance to change." Two CEOs stated the problem more forcefully
and from different perspectives:

> Ninety percent of the people in the bank today entered the in-
> dustry to not do the things they have to do now. And somehow
> I'm supposed to get them to change.

> I'm very frustrated with the officers returning from graduate
> banking programs. They don't seem to come back wanting to
> change things, or telling me what I'm doing wrong, asking the
> questions they should be asking. I want to know who wants my
> job—and I'm afraid no one does.

*Developing Responsive Organization Structures.* One
of the biggest barriers to change and successful strategy implementation in most banks is the present organization structure.
But most bank managers have not identified the culprit. Instead, they state their most important problems to be:

- Departments that can't get along.
- The inability to implement quickly.
- The inability to develop new products and services in a
  timely manner.
- Conflicts between departments that compete instead of
  cooperate.

They admit their bank is not a responsive, flexible organization
that can move quickly when it has to. But they often see people

as the culprit. They explain personality clashes between groups, uncommitted or unmotivated employees, and turf battles as natural occurrences in a bank.

Such symptoms are usually clear indicators of problems with the bank's organization structure. The best bank managers know that how the bank is structured is a major influence on how employees behave at work and on what they think is right, expected, important, and rewarded.

### 4. Creating Banks that Can Cope with Change Requires that Bank Managers Themselves Be the First Targets of Change

Change is a certainty in a deregulated industry. Adapting to perpetual change requires flexible, responsive banking organizations. Managing change will require more than moving the bank from one stable condition through a turbulent transition to another stable condition. Today it means managing in a condition of "constant whitewater," no small challenge for an industry where most managers were trained to navigate in continuously blue water.

One of the most important, although subtle, findings of our research is this: The best bank managers understand that they must begin the process of change with themselves and conclude with the people who do the work. They *never* ask the people who do the work to create change. One CEO stated this important point well when he said:

> The behavior of the people in this bank mirrors my behavior in many respects. If I believe they need to change, then how can I exempt myself?

Less-effective bank managers begin implementing change with the people who do the work and then change themselves. Belatedly, they recognize the need to change their own behavior. The best bank managers seem to know that developing bank strategy is an "outside → in" process, while the changes necessary to implement new strategy involve an "inside → out" process that begins with themselves.

## 5. The Set of Skills Required to Be an Effective Bank Manager Has Enlarged and the Mix of the Three Skills within the Set Has Shifted.

If the components of the managerial job in banking have changed, it follows that the skills required to do the job effectively have also changed. Being effective as a bank manager requires a set of three broad skills: technical, conceptual, and human.[2]

*Technical skill* is the most familiar skill in the industry because it has always been the most important and required of the largest number of people. It involves specialized knowledge and analytical tools within a particular banking specialty. It also involves the capability to use those tools.

Most banking educational programs and in-bank training focus almost entirely on the development of *technical banking skills* such as asset-liability management, commercial lending, installment lending, and investment and trust administration, and on the development of *technical functional skills* such as marketing, human resource administration, and investment analysis.

Bank managers must be technically proficient, of course. It will be a challenge for banking educational programs just to keep their curriculums current in technical skills. However, we found that managing the bank will also depend on certain conceptual and human skills as the management and leadership components of the bank manager's job enlarge.

*Conceptual skill* involves the ability to see the big picture and deal with high levels of abstract reasoning and analyses. Bankers must deal daily with abstract concepts, including dynamic economic, technological, regulatory, and competitive forces, and new ideas. But effective managers must "read" what parts of the environment are of strategic importance to their bank or part of the bank, and create a vision that relates the bank or unit to that environment. Then they must develop and sustain a culture that shares the vision by clearly communicating it throughout the bank or unit. To do so calls for skill in strategic analysis, organizational design, and managing change.

Yet the career paths of most bankers typically provide little hands-on experience with this kind of abstraction. The conditions of the industry prior to deregulation focused attention on immediate, short-run, "next-quarter" concerns. Little opportunity existed for a banker to develop conceptual skills.

*Human skill* is the ability to be effective interpersonally, as well as the ability to be an effective team builder and team member. The often-heard expression, "banking is a people business," relays the increasing importance of people skills in banking. There is no disagreement on the importance of people skills as essential to bank performance. The skill influences the manager's relationships not only with subordinates, but also with peers, superiors, customers, and external groups. It requires specific skills in leadership, team building, communication, and decision making.

While more skills are needed for bank managers to be effective, the relative importance of the skill mix has also shifted. The bankers with whom we spoke made it clear that conceptual skills and human skills are equally as important as technical skills today, and furthermore, they will provide the competitive advantage in the future.

## INTRODUCING *THE NEW BANKER*

*The New Banker* was written in a dynamic era in the banking industry as we continue to move toward a much different and still uncertain future. The problems and complexities our industry will confront during this era cannot be solved by time or evolution. This era calls for effective management and leadership.

As we shall see throughout the book, there are bank managers who have created changes in their organizations or units, gained the commitment of employees, and sustained new cultures, and who are developing innovative organization structures. They have done things in new ways and they are succeeding. They are bankers/managers/leaders.

# PART 2

# DEVELOPING A PERFORMANCE CULTURE

There are no bad regiments, only bad colonels.

*Napoleon Bonaparte*

# CHAPTER 2

---

# THE PEOPLE CHALLENGE: ACCELERATING PEAK PERFORMANCE

---

*You just set the work before the men and have them do it.*

Henry Ford

Think of an outstanding experience you had recently in a bank, hotel, health-care organization, retail store, or with an airline or rental car agency. It was the kind of experience when you thought to yourself later, I'm going to get that person's name and write a letter to the company telling them what a great employee they have. This chapter provides actual episodes of peak performances. As we review them, the question we want to ask is, What do all of these peak performances have in common? Understanding the answer to this question will provide the challenge that bankers face as they seek to develop high-performance cultures. We are looking for the common denominator of peak performance.

### Working the Night Shift

In spite of constant encouragement throughout the year by his accountant, a man realized on December 31 that he had not opened the Keogh Plan that the accountant had told him to open. He called the bank where he had his checking account and was told, "You should have come in earlier in the year." A friend recommended a private banker at another bank who would surely understand his plight and find time to help him. He called her and explained apologetically how critical it was for him to get the account opened since this was the last day of the year. Her reply was, "Who gave you my number?"

On the third try at another bank he was told by a trust officer that it was impossible to meet because he had appointments throughout the day. The customer thanked him for his time and was about to hang up when he said, "What are you doing tonight?" The happy ending to the episode is that the banker made a special trip to his office that evening at 7:30 and spent one and one-half hours with the customer covering every aspect of the Keogh Plan.

### Freshly Popped, Piping Hot Service

An air traveler boarded a flight in Seattle bound for Lexington, Kentucky. During the Seattle to Portland portion he snacked on peanuts. More peanuts followed on the Portland to Dallas portion. As the time zones changed, his desire for more substantial food increased. He was sure that the change of planes in Dallas for the flight to Atlanta would bring with it a meal. Unfortunately, because of another time zone change, it was now late afternoon and only peanuts were served.

Between Dallas and Atlanta the desperately hungry passenger kept his thoughts on the popcorn he would buy at the Atlanta airport before boarding his flight to Lexington. Arriving a little late in Atlanta, he hurried to the gate for the flight to Lexington which was boarding when he reached it. After checking in, he turned toward the snack area only to find an empty, closed-up popcorn machine. He lamented to the gate agent how hungry he was. The agent said that only peanuts would be served on the flight.

Sitting in his seat on the plane, he resigned himself to the fact that he would have to wait for something to eat. Just as the door was about to close, the gate agent came on the plane carrying a freshly popped, piping hot bag of microwave popcorn. He had gone to the flight crew lounge which was equipped with a microwave oven and popcorn for use by flight crews between flights, and prepared the snack for the hungry passenger.

### When Life Gives You Lemons, Make Lemonade

It was a record-breaking heat wave and this particular Friday afternoon had broken all the previous records. Cars were lined up 10 and 12 deep at each of the bank's drive-in lanes. Patience was in short supply and tempers were flaring. The branch personnel were under the usual pressure and had to deal with edgy customers as well.

The branch manager took the initiative. He went to a nearby supermarket and purchased several cans of frozen lemonade and numerous bags of ice and cups. He returned to the branch and mixed up a large amount of lemonade which he served to the branch staff. He then left the building and personally served lemonade to the waiting customers as they sat in their cars.

The three episodes each illustrate a peak performance. But before bank managers can undertake ways to encourage such behavior, we must first understand what constitutes peak performance. Dissecting the above episodes will provide us the answer.

## WHAT IS PEAK PERFORMANCE?

In the mid-1980s, the Public Agenda Foundation found that fewer than one out of four jobholders (23 percent) in America say they are currently working at their full potential.[1] Nearly half of all jobholders (44 percent) say that they do not put much effort into their jobs over and above what is required to hold on to the job. Finally, close to 6 out of 10 working Americans (62 percent) believe that "most people do not work as hard as they used to."

If the majority of people in your bank are like those surveyed above, they are operating on minimums. The people in the three episodes were operating on maximums.

What do all peak performances seem to have in common? Examining the three episodes is revealing. It is important to note that in each one, the employee *chose to do* what they did; they did not *have to do* what they did. The trust officer, ramp agent, and branch manager would still have their jobs today at the same level of salary if they had chosen *not* to do what they did.

The same critical point applies to your own peak-performance episodes. More than likely, no matter what kind of experience you had, the employee chose to perform at that moment far beyond what was necessary. No one was supervising them, no one was looking over their shoulder. But when the need arose they voted for the company and the customer, not for themselves.

After such experiences, bankers often say, "Why can't I get the people in my department to do this?" or "Why can't the employees at our bank be like this?" Bank managers know they want it, and need it. They know they must get better results from people. They can even point to it ("I wish my people would do that"). However, when asked to define "it," most bankers in our study said something like, "I don't know what it is but I know it when I see it."

## The Components of a Peak Performance

The foundation of all peak performance and the development of a performance culture in any bank is *discretionary effort*. It's the difference between the maximum amount of care and effort a person brings to the job and the minimum amount necessary to keep from being penalized or reprimanded [2] Discretionary effort has always been with us but for bankers it was never as important as it is now Thus, we propose the following formula for peak performance:

### The Peak-Performance Formula

$$\text{Acceptable performance} + \text{Discretionary effort} = \text{Peak performance}$$

Returning to the peak-performance episodes, the trust officer, ramp agent, and branch manager became peak performers when what each of them did required discretionary effort:

- The "choose-to-do" part of their job versus the "have-to-do" part of their job (acceptable performance)
- The difference between the maximum possible and the minimum acceptable
- The difference between what we are and what we know we can be

### Banks Sell Human Performances

Discretionary effort is the common denominator of peak performance. It is also a critical concept for bank managers whose
goal is to develop a high-performance culture in their bank or
unit.

Bank managers often pay lip service to the idea that banking is a people business, but the pivotal difference between a
bank and an organization that produces goods is that:

1. Banks do not produce—they perform.
2. Banks do not sell things—they sell human performances.

These performances are often labor intensive, which means
that human efforts constitute the actual "product" that customers buy. If the human efforts are responsive and competent,
then the product is responsive and competent. If the human efforts are unresponsive and incompetent, then the product is
unresponsive and incompetent. The majority of complaints that
come into GM are not aimed at people—they are aimed at
products. The majority of complaints that come into a bank are
not aimed at products—they are aimed at people. All this simply means is that a rude CSR on a given day is a rude bank. An
incompetent and unprepared calling officer is an incompetent
bank.

---

The common denominator of peak performance is discretionary
effort.

---

Many people assume that the electronic banking move-
ment will diminish the role and importance of people in banking, especially retail banking. As machines do more, people
will do less, or so the theory goes. The theory is wrong. In the
best-managed banks, machines will do more, but so will people.
There may be fewer people in certain types of jobs, and they
may be different kinds of people than were hired heretofore,
but they will do more and be more important to the success of

the bank than ever before.[3] Banking has changed and the work force of banking has permanently changed as a result.

## THE CHANGING BANKING WORK FORCE

It is safe to say that in preregulation days, the majority of jobs in a bank were low-discretion jobs. The jobholder had little discretion or control over how much or how little effort was devoted to his or her work.[4] This structure was a key to the success of assembly line production industries and assumes that jobs can be broken down into simple tasks easily timed and paced. It reduces reliance on individual commitment, motivation, and creativity by reducing individual discretion in the job.

Success in banking before deregulation was not found in upgrading the skills and knowledge of frontline employees but by simplifying the jobs of tellers, loan officers, and cashiers. Banks followed the low-discretion model—seeking to maximize productivity by minimizing discretion, and therefore, the need for commitment, initiative, creativity, and motivation on the part of individual employees. And management sought to hire people who fit that model.

The bank's organization structure was a highly centralized one with highly specialized jobs, and a strict hierarchical system of authority with layers of management. There was an implicit assumption that people could be supervised into being effective and that management was more critical to the success of the bank than individual jobholders.

But that was yesterday. Today's bank is dominated by high-discretion jobs. The jobholder has a great amount of discretion or control over how much or how little effort is devoted to work. Calling officers, customer service representatives (CSRs), relationship managers, sales personnel, branch managers, trust bankers, private bankers, product managers, and sales managers have a great deal of control over their levels of effort on the job. They are part of the new "knowledge workers" and have increased the total amount of discretion in the banking workplace. Their jobs are knowledge-intensive and require skilled and educated people. These people are also critical to the success of today's bank. And high performance in a high-discretion job requires individual commitment and motivation. Unlike the old bank work force, the new bank work force cannot be supervised into being effective. An unmotivated person in a high-discretion job is an unmotivated organization while an unmotivated person in a low-discretion job probably has little negative impact on the organization. As one senior vice president of retail banking put it:

> We can no longer afford to employ the very kinds of people we used to consciously seek to hire.

Perhaps one CEO put it best when he said:

> We used to look for experience; now we look for brains.

Unfortunately, in many banks, managerial skills have not kept pace with the changes in the bank's work force. Many banks have individuals in management positions who came out of low-discretion jobs, who are using low-discretion management and supervisory techniques trying to manage people in high-discretion jobs. The same CEO noted:

> We are being forced to throw away the old tradition. We don't have time to move people from the bottom to the top. Today we have to go out and get managers who are ready to go.

Because the composition of the work force is ahead of the managerial practices in many banks, the behavior of many middle managers in these banks hinders rather than helps the move to a performance culture. When the bank was a low-discretion workplace, such behavior by middle managers probably did little damage—at least to the bank. Such managerial practices in a high-discretion workplace can be disastrous. One CEO summarized the problem well when he said:

> The trouble with having to always tell people what to do is that it is all they will do.

If the composition of the banking work force has changed, then the job of managing people in a bank has also changed. As hard as bankers might try, they cannot depersonalize the new banking with old banking management techniques using industrial-oriented models of production. The new banking is not a business of tasks and tools, or of process and procedure. It is much more. It is a business based on human performance and interaction. Smokestack industry-management techniques are no longer applicable.

---

In the best-managed banks, machines will do more, but so will people.

---

In the old banking, management could control performance and tighten control measures while ignoring such factors as commitment and motivation because such intangibles made little difference. The opposite is true today. Bank managers must influence, however indirectly, commitment and motivation because it is these intangibles the bank needs if it is to perform at the level it must to survive and prosper.

## THE REALITIES AND MANAGEMENT CHALLENGES OF THE NEW BANKING WORK FORCE

The management challenges of the high-discretion job are presented clearly in Figure 2–1 which illustrates the discretionary component of some selected jobs in a typical bank. What are the important managerial implications of discretionary effort?

### Realities for Management

There are three realities of discretionary effort:[5]
    **1.** *It is that portion of an employee's effort over which he or she has the greatest control.* Discretionary effort is like discretionary income. We do not have to spend it if we do not wish to. And if we decide to spend it, we determine when, where, how, and how much of it we will spend. In each of our peak-performance episodes, the trust officer, ramp agent, and branch manager made a personal decision to spend it

**FIGURE 2-1**
**Discretionary Effort Component for Selected Jobs**

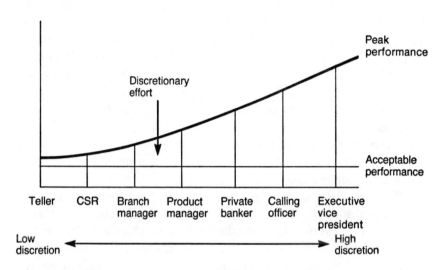

**2.** *It is that part of an employee's performance that management cannot control.* This is a critical point. Management can control the *acceptable performance* part of the peak-performance formula. In a low-discretion job this is the largest contributor to peak performance. However, for high-discretion jobs acceptable performance is the smallest contributor. Management can *control* acceptable performance. It can only *influence* discretionary effort.

**3.** *Jobs highest in discretionary effort are customer contact jobs and knowledge jobs.* Banking is an information business. Banking jobs are knowledge jobs and/or customer contact jobs. The new jobs in banking are all high-discretion jobs.

## Challenges for Management

The implications of the concept of discretionary effort present some critical challenges to bank managers based on the following realities:

**1.** *The most important parts of employees' contributions to the goals of your bank or unit are being made at their discretion.* Airlines can measure and control on-time landings and baggage mishaps. Bankers can measure and control how many times a phone rings before it is answered, whether employees smile, call customers by name, are out-of-balance, or make their officer calls. Unfortunately, this is only acceptable performance. Customers expect their statements to be correct and on time. They expect courtesy. Airline passengers expect flights to be on time and their baggage to arrive when they do. However, airlines cannot direct that ramp agents make popcorn or pilots help an elderly person put away their luggage. A bank cannot put into the job description of branch managers that they must make lemonade or that trust officers must work at night. But it is these discretionary acts that constitute a peak performance and a true performance culture.

   **2.** *Encouraging peak performance in your bank or unit involves getting employees to do things they don't have to do if they don't want to.* When the employee has to choose between the bank or customer and themselves, which one will prevail? Management is not looking over their shoulder. The called-for action is not part of their job description. They do not *have to* do it. If they *choose to* do it, if they vote for the bank or customer, you have a performance culture.

   **3.** *Encouraging peak performance in your bank or unit involves getting employees to spend something they never had to spend before.* Very simply, it is management's responsibility to communicate in words as well as deeds that when you are in a service business a basic truth prevails: "When your services are the same—you will win or lose on the performances of your people." If this truth is understood and accepted, another one logically follows: "Acceptable performance is no longer acceptable." The ticket into the ballpark is acceptable performance. The winner's edge will go to those banks where peak performance is the only acceptable performance.

   **4.** *Managers can enforce acceptable performance but leadership is needed to unleash discretionary effort.* In many respects, prior to deregulation acceptable performance was peak performance. This is because as already noted, an unmotivated person in a low-discretion job probably has little negative impact on the bank.

Unlike the old bank work force, the new work force cannot be supervised into being effective.

Banks can still enforce or police acceptable performance for high-discretion jobs. But because of the possibility of so many variations in circumstances that can occur at the front line, acceptable performance is only a small part of what the individual is capable of for a high-discretion job. Loan officers, trust officers, private bankers, and CSRs are not interchangeable parts in a machine. Leadership is what banks need if all employees are to willingly seek the maximum possible when the circumstances call for it.

    **5.** *Authority can produce acceptable performance, but only commitment produces discretionary effort.* And in the age of an increasingly educated work force, the commitment may not be to the bank—but to the job. We met many bank officers who were committed to be the best they could be at what they did. Management must foster the conditions which allow both commitment to the bank as well as to the job

## ACHIEVING PEAK PERFORMANCE

Individual discretionary effort is a necessary condition for a performance culture. High-discretion employees doing their best work requires discretionary effort. Thus, bank managers desiring a performance culture must consider ways for encouraging peak performance. They must also avoid doing things that discourage discretionary effort.

### Encouraging Peak Performance

Many individuals think of the difference between the maximum possible and the minimum acceptable as a commitment gap. Such gaps exist when people operate at minimum levels because they do not have commitment to their job or to the organization.

It is becoming clear that the low-discretion model is out of step with today's knowledge workers. These educated people want the satisfaction of knowing that their work is competent and respected. Unfortunately, many banking organizations are not structured to provide that level of satisfaction. (It is not surprising, therefore, that building responsive organization structures was identified in our research as a major management challenge.)

What do knowledge workers want from their jobs? The Public Agenda Foundation found these top 10 qualities people want in a job today:[6]

1. Working with people who treat me with respect.
2. Interesting work.
3. Recognition for good work.
4. Chance to develop skills.
5. Working with people who listen if you have ideas about how to do things better.
6. A chance to think for myself rather than just carry out instructions.
7. Seeing the end results of my work.
8. Working for efficient managers.
9. A job that is not too easy.
10. Feeling well informed about what is going on.

For bank managers, it is interesting to note that job security, benefits, and high pay did not make the top 10 (although they were in the top 15). Yet many bank managers who follow the low-discretion model still deal with people as if security, benefits, and money are the only ways to encourage peak performance.

It is somewhat ironic that some bank managers continue to use security, benefits, and money when the rewards that people want—opportunity for growth, challenge, respect, being informed, and participation—are what banking needs to gain the commitment of people to their jobs and to the bank. As one senior retail banker stated:

It is management's responsibility to make employees want to do more than show up for work.

A true performance culture is one in which everyone does their best work, and it is management's responsibility to create the conditions where everyone is able to do their best work. The following five management actions will succeed in encouraging individual commitment and peak performance:[7]

- Managers should tie remuneration directly to performance that enhances both the efficiency and effectiveness of the bank or unit.
- Managers should give public and tangible recognition to people who perform beyond the acceptable level. The branch manager and trust officer who opened this chapter should be heroes at their institutions and management should make them so.
- Top management must accept wholeheartedly the principle that employees should share directly and significantly in overall productivity gains (however defined).
- Managers should encourage employees to participate with management in defining recognizable goals and standards against which individual performance can be judged.
- Top management should give special attention to the problems and difficulties that middle managers face in supporting and implementing programs of change in the bank.

## Discouraging Peak Performance

As banks move away from being low-discretion workplaces and begin to do the things required of the high-discretion workplace, some managers may be called upon to exhibit competence and skill in areas of managing people where these were not previously demanded. Under such circumstances, managers, out of frustration, desperation, or poor advice, may be tempted to do something that is risky and has little chance for success—or worse, causes great damage. Bank managers should be cautious about doing any of the following:[8]

- Permitting situations to develop where the interests of employees run counter to the well-being of the bank. For example, by introducing new technology in a way that threatens employees' job security or overtime; by introducing incentive pay systems that exclude groups whose efforts are needed to complete the transaction; or by pitting one group against another who are involved in serving the same customer group.
- Trying to improve productivity or quality of service and not being prepared to accept the costs of such programs.
- Permitting a significant gap to develop between management rhetoric and the bank's actual reward system. Nothing feeds employee cynicism more than management blindness about which behaviors are really important.
- Pretending or trying to mislead employees into believing that programs designed to increase productivity are actually intended to increase job satisfaction and employee morale; nothing breeds a greater mistrust of management.
- Providing special perks, bonuses, or privileges for managers that widen the gap between them and those who do the work—for example, providing management bonuses when some employees are being laid off.

## LESSONS IN PEAK PERFORMANCE FROM OTHER INDUSTRIES

Like most people, we experience acceptable or less than acceptable performances from service organizations daily. Occasionally we experience a peak performance like those at the beginning of the chapter. But being both recipients of peak performance and students of peak performance makes each encounter a mini-laboratory for us.

We get to live what we study. For the purpose of this book, one of the authors kept a diary of performance episodes which, like those which opened the chapter, were valuable learning experiences. The ones reported in this section document episodes in other industries but the lessons from them have a great deal of relevance for improving individual performance in banks.[9]

The first lesson took place when checking into an Alabama gulf coast hotel at 1 A.M. for one night. He was up at 6 A.M. to attend an early breakfast meeting and returned to his room at 10 A.M. to pack. At noon he returned to get his luggage, and the message light was flashing. The operator told him that the message had come in at 8 P.M. the previous evening.

Upon checking out, he mentioned to the front desk manager what had happened. He was not looking for a complimentary meal or box of candy since he was on his way to the airport. He simply assumed that she would or should want to know.

She did not apologize on behalf of the hotel. "I do not answer the phones, sir. What time did you check in?" she asked instead. "About 1 A.M.," he replied. She explained that the personnel who do that job leave at about 11 P.M.

When he told her that the light was not on in the morning, she said, "They don't come to work until around 8 A.M." When he told her that he returned to his room at 10 A.M., and the light was not on, she said, "You probably didn't see it. Sometimes they are difficult to see during the day." **1. Peak performance means never having to say, "That's not my job."**

What was of particular interest in this encounter is that not only did the manager tell the customer it was not her job, she tried to tell him it was his job. Undoubtedly fresh out of an assertiveness-training course, she had him explaining his own behavior.

According to her, he did not get the message because he got in too late, got up too early, and cannot see very well. But in the process, she taught him another more subtle lesson about peak performance. **2. Peak performance is never the customer's job.**

The third lesson emerged last summer, when he went to buy 1,000 25-cent stamps. He asked the man at the counter for 10 rolls of 25-cent stamps and counted out $250.

After looking in his drawer, the employee said he could only give him sheets. The customer explained that sheets would cause a great deal of unnecessary work for his assistant and that rolls were exactly what he needed and wanted. The employee said that if he sold him 10 rolls he would have none left in his drawer. "That's great," the customer said. "You're having a good day. You've sold out."

"No," he said, it was policy that he could not sell all of his rolls because he would not have any for other customers later in his shift. The customer noted that a recurring fantasy of every businessperson he knew was to sell out. When that didn't work he suggested that he buy four rolls, come back later (perhaps in disguise) and buy three more, and so on. As he climbed into his car with 1,000 stamps in sheets, he realized he had just learned another lesson about peak performance. **3. Peak performers never inconvenience customers because of company policies that are known only to employees—and do not become known to customers until they are used against them.**

This lesson has been repeated several times since. Recently, he fell in love with a sweater displayed in a store window in Chicago. Unfortunately, the store was out of stock in all sizes. "It might be hard to reach," he said, "but the one in the window is my size." The salesperson informed him that it was company policy not to take anything out of the window.

He tried to explain that since there were none in stock in any size, all this policy could possibly result in was one lost sale and more disappointed customers like himself. And she could avoid all of these problems by selling him the sweater. He is learning to live without the sweater.

Unfortunately, as in the above two cases, more often than not the "policies" make absolutely no sense to the customer and the organization gets the blame. More likely than not, the policies are invented on the spot at the convenience of employees to avoid additional work. That is, at that moment, the employee makes a decision not to spend any discretionary effort and the customer and the organization both lose.

The fourth lesson came about on the second morning of a 13-night stay in a Seattle motel. He reached for the shampoo while in the shower and couldn't find any. He got out and called the desk to ask for some to be sent up. He was asked by the desk clerk when he checked in. "What difference does that make?" he inquired.

The desk clerk informed him that it was hotel policy to give guests shampoo only on their first night. He said he had never heard of a business that does less for a customer the more they spend and that the policy only made sense if they were promoting one nighters.

He was then passed on to the assistant front desk manager, and finally to the front desk manager. Any hope of getting shampoo was lost when he suggested that he would check out every morning and check back in every night for 13 nights. In this way he would be consistent with company policy and also get some shampoo. It was suggested that he find another hotel.

This incredible episode is, of course, another excellent example of lesson 3. The guest was never informed of the policy when he checked in and it makes absolutely no sense. He found out about it when an employee used it against him as he stood dripping wet in the middle of his hotel room. However, it taught him another lesson about peak performance. **4. A peak performer never requires a customer to restate his or her request or problem to several people.**

He learned his fifth lesson when he and his wife had an early dinner at a very fine restaurant. Being early, they were alone and struck up an immediate friendship with the waitress with whom they chatted throughout their meal. Another couple came in near the end of their meal and ordered a Caesar salad with their meal. The waitress rolled the cart close to his table and continued chatting while she prepared the salad for the second couple.

"This is the first Caesar salad I've ever made," she said. He saw some squirming at the other table. "In fact," she said, "I had never even heard of one until I started working here. But I watched my manager make one last week and snuck a leaf out of the bowl to taste it." Now he began to squirm. She delivered the salads and returned to the kitchen. Within 30 seconds, he heard the woman at the next table say, "This is the worst Caesar salad I've ever had in my life."

He thought of this encounter recently on a short flight on

his least favorite airline. When the flight attendants were passing out snacks, they ran out just as they got to him. He said he understood, as the attendant apologized. Then she added, "What do you expect from XYZ Airlines?" **5. If you establish negative expectations for your customers, you will always meet them.**

His sixth lesson occurred in a hospital. His mother who had a stroke 10 days earlier was transferred by ambulance from a hospital to a rehabilitation facility 50 miles away. She sat in a wheelchair in the lobby of the rehabilitation facility for almost three hours. She was denied admission because the hospital had not properly completed the necessary documentation. She was transported by ambulance 50 miles back to the hospital.

He inquired about the circumstances surrounding this incredible performance asking only two questions: (1) What happened? and (2) Who was responsible? In separate conversations with five key personnel, each blamed the other, several commented on the inadequacies and incompetencies of the others, and not one made a supportive comment about any of the others. **6. You can never treat customers any better than you treat each other.**

There is a very important truth in this lesson for bank managers. It is that in a service business, how an employee feels is more likely than not how the customer will eventually feel. We may issue instructions on how employees are to dress and behave. But we cannot instruct them on how to feel. And how they feel will usually surface in how they behave.

The final lesson was imparted in a department store when he went to buy a pot. It was a huge and rather expensive pot, and he had a question he needed answered. He could see the salesperson was on the phone with a customer, so he waited about 10 minutes. When she hung up she came toward him but didn't say, "May I help you?" or "Sorry to keep you waiting." He was about to ask his question when she said, "You wouldn't believe the stupid questions customers ask." Having learned his other lessons well, he told her he did not need any help, thanked her, and left the store. **7. A great many customers will not return poor performance with bad behavior.**

**They are always polite and never get loud, cause a scene, or scream for the manager. They just never come back.**

It should be clear that we believe that *no* competitive weapon is more important to a bank today and tomorrow than the quality of its people. One way to compete in this kind of environment is to have the finest caliber of people—people who give the maximum discretionary effort, who like those individuals early in this chapter, make the bank easy to do business with. Machines can provide informational and transactional convenience, but only people can provide the credibility, competence, creativity, and care that build long-term customer and client relationships.

# CHAPTER 3

## LEADING YOURSELF AND OTHERS: FOUR ESSENTIAL STRATEGIES

*We go where our vision is.*
Joseph Murphy

Ask any group of senior bank officers anywhere in the country if during the last year they have ever thought, Where is my bank headed? At least 90 percent of them will immediately raise their hands. Ask them if they ever wonder, Why does my bank seem to be drifting? and 80 to 90 percent will raise their hands.

Actually, such thoughts tell us a great deal. When you have such questions about your bank, you are actually putting management on trial. For these thoughts cut directly to the heart of a problem. They are questions about your bank's lack of direction, leadership, strategy, and vision.

The best bank managers know where their banks or part of the bank is going. In many banks, of course, this is far from reality. It is in these banks that managers continually wonder where the bank is headed, and why departments continually compete so well with each other while the bank itself has trouble competing in the marketplace.

This chapter examines four important practices that contribute to the success of effective bank managers as they strive to create a performance culture in their banks. These practices are not quick fixes and in many instances, they are not visible to others. In fact, effective bank managers are not always consciously aware of these practices; they view them as "just some-

thing that I do." But they are important contributors to suc
cess. There are undoubtedly others, but these four appear to be
particularly important to effective bank managers:

1. They create visions of greatness.
2. They separate the problems of their job from the conditions of their job.
3. They believe that what they do is at least as important
   as what they plan to do.
4. They develop strategic responses to change.

## CREATING A VISION

We have known for many years that visualization is apparently a successful means of individual motivation. Psychologists and human potential experts are pretty much convinced
that people who set a goal and repeatedly visualize its accomplishment often achieve great things.[1]

They tell us that envisioning our goals, writing them
down, constantly referring to them throughout the day, and re-
hearsing our future is a self-development technique practiced
by many achievement-oriented individuals as a method of self-
motivation.

As a result of our research for this book, we have become
convinced that such techniques also may be applicable to
groups, and thus could be useful to those bank managers who
are faced with the task of getting better results from
people—and fast. We found that more often than not, the best
bank managers utilize visualization or some variation of it in
their work.

Most of the CEOs had left the room after an intensive focus
group interview in which the majority of the discussion had
centered on the problems and difficulties of getting the best efforts of people. One CEO remained behind, however, to show us
something he had in his wallet. It was a three-by-five-inch
folded index card on which he had typed: "We will become the
best bank in the state for medium-size businesses by 1992."

Another time we were visiting a bank branch when the newly
appointed branch manager, a former student, called us into her

office. After talking over old times, she opened the top drawer of her desk. Taped to the bottom of the drawer was the following: "The service we provide the customers of our branch will be demonstrably better than any branch of any bank in the city."

We also visited the operations area of a brokerage firm. No one in the department ever met face-to-face with clients. We were surprised when we looked up behind a desk and found a framed statement that read: "We deliver client-driven service that is unparalleled by any firm in any industry in the world."

In his best-selling book *Megatrends: Ten New Directions Transforming Our Lives*, John Naisbett discusses the concept of a "vision." In fact, he argues that "strategic planning is worthless unless there is first a strategic vision . . . a clear image of what you want to achieve, which then organizes and instructs every step toward that goal."[2] We found that the most effective bank managers have an image, a vision, of exactly what they want to achieve.

What is a vision of greatness? Listening to the best bank managers leads us to believe it is at least two things:

- A clear image or picture of what you want your bank or unit of the bank to be.
- A focus on what you want to achieve—not necessarily how it will be achieved.

This clear image of a goal is then used to organize and instruct every step toward its achievement. Note that the above three visions of greatness qualify on each dimension. They focus on what the business or unit wants to be and provide very clear direction for managerial decision making.

Effective bank managers know that their bank is headed somewhere. It almost certainly has momentum. If they do not consciously set the direction, then the direction or momentum must evolve out of everyday operating decisions. In fact, the direction will be nothing more than the sum total of the day-to-day operating decisions.

## Creating Your Vision

In creating a vision there are guideposts. Among those bankers with whom we have worked, three predictors of success appear repeatedly:

- Make it achievable.
- Make it motivational.
- Make it a crusade for customers.

*Achievable.*  By acting on their view of what is possible, and with a clear sense of purpose, the best bank managers seek to create a work environment in which other people can share their commitment, and where commitment is the norm, not the exception. But, while the vision should "stretch" the bank or unit toward more effective performance, it must, at the same time, be realistic and achievable. In other words, it should open a vision of new opportunities of what could be, but becoming "the best bank in the state for medium-size businesses" should not lead the bank into unrealistic ventures far beyond its capabilities.

*Motivational.*  There seems to be unanimous belief in the motivational power of a vision of greatness. Apparently the image that such a vision creates, inspires action and fuels motivation. One of the most important benefits of a vision, which was consistently supported in our interviews, is the motivation it provides other managers and employees of the bank or unit. It provides a shared sense of purpose outside the day-to-day activities taking place within the bank or unit. Therefore, such end results as ROA, new business, cross-sell ratios, and reduction in closed accounts can then be viewed as the result of the pursuit and achievement of a vision and not the vision itself. Otherwise, the numbers are the vision. When we asked the CEO what purpose his index card served, he replied, "It tells me and everyone else in the bank why we get up and come to work in the morning."

*A Crusade for Customers.*    Customers should be critical in determining the vision. The best statements of vision do not mention end results such as ROA, profits, cross-sell ratios, costs, or the bottom line. Many managers make them "crusades" for the customer, a cause with an impact that is beyond the personal goals and desires of employees and that is worth pursuing for its own sake. Commenting on her vision of service the branch manager stated, "The only reward most bank employees usually get for all their efforts is that the bank makes more money. I believe people want to commit to something bigger, at least I do."

Finally, the head of a private banking department shared his vision: "We are committed to the success of our clients and view them as partners." There can be no doubt that the efforts of employees are an important competitive weapon for a bank The possibility always exists that a competitor will offer to pay more for deposits or take less for loans. One way to compete in such an environment is to have employees who are willing to go the extra mile for the bank or the customer when the extra mile is needed.

---

If management does not consciously set direction then it will become nothing more than the sum total of day-to-day operating decisions.

---

## Communicating Your Vision

The interpersonal skill of communication is important in build ing support for your vision. Leadership is keeping others focused on the vision. One way to do this is to get people comfort able talking about it. In his book *The Empowered Manager*, Peter Block outlines four ways to help command others' interest when communicating your vision.[3]

*Optimism.*    Since your vision is your statement of a preferred future, talking about it with conviction and enthusiasm will always be persuasive

***Emotional Charge.*** You should use color and excitement in your language. Words such as greatness, service, meaning, integrity, and perfection, are emotionally charged words that people can get excited about. Such words helped the branch manager focus on a deeper set of values than simply costs and productivity.

***Metaphors.*** To help others get a picture of your vision, use metaphors, parables, and picture images. The sports and war metaphors have always been popular. They are often used to promote ideas of teamwork, quarterback leadership, and competitive spirit. However, others have successfully used trees, orchestras, machinery, airplanes, and the four seasons.

***Specific Picture of the Future.*** The more people can see what the future would look like, the easier it is for them to understand and communicate it to others. When President John F. Kennedy declared, "We will put a man on the moon before the end of the decade," all Americans clearly understood his picture of the future, and thousands of government employees couldn't wait to get up the next day to go help make it a reality

These four qualities of a vision statement help to communicate it to others. Talking about your vision in a vivid way also encourages other people to do the same. Let's review the four statements of vision we have referred to in this section. Note that they measure well in terms of communicating themselves effectively·

- "We will become the best bank in the state for medium-size businesses by 1992."
- "The service we provide the customers of our branch will be demonstrably better than any branch of any bank in the city."
- "We deliver client-driven service that is unparalleled by any firm in any industry in the world."
- "We are committed to the success of our clients and view them as partners."

## SEPARATING PROBLEMS FROM CONDITIONS

The best bank managers have a skill that is very important for physicians and is also essential for bank managers in today's dynamic environment. What is that skill? It is the ability to separate the problems of their job from the conditions of their job.[4]

Sometime during their training, physicians learn to classify the situations they face into one of two categories: (1) those that can be cured or fixed, and (2) those that cannot be cured or fixed. This skill enables them to then bring the appropriate expertise to bear on each category, thereby maximizing their contribution to the patients' well-being.

A physician determines quickly whether a patient has a medical problem or a medical condition. A problem could be a broken bone, appendicitis, or tonsillitis. A condition could be allergies, chronic sinusitis, and certain skin disorders.

The distinction between a problem and a condition is an important one to a physician. Medical problems can be cured or fixed. The physician may have to review several possible complex solutions with long and involved recuperation times, but once a cure is selected the physician knows with a high degree of certainty what the outcome will be. After the necessary recuperation time, everything will be basically as it was before the problem arose.

For a condition, however, the physician knows that it cannot be cured or fixed. Both the physician and the patient also know that everything will never be as it was before the situation arose. The physician does not try to cure or fix the condition. Instead, he or she "treats" the condition often with the help of the patient. Together they try to maintain a delicate balance so the patient can function normally. Very importantly, a physician never tries to cure a medical condition because he or she knows that conditions cannot be cured and that trying to do so is a waste of both time and money.

### Banking and Medicine

This idea is a very useful one for the best bank managers. When the industry was regulated, the majority of situations bank managers faced were problems. Examples include complying with regulations, locating a branch, and making loan decisions. Like medical problems, solving banking problems might take time, require a great deal of analysis, and be quite complex. But once the solution was decided upon, the decision made, the branch site selected, the loan granted or not granted, the problem was solved. The banker moved on to the next problem.

In other words, *prior to deregulation, bankers were primarily problem solvers.* The majority of the situations we faced had solutions or at least specific endpoints where decisions had to be made. Today it's different. Bankers face even more complex banking problems but they also face situations they never faced before deregulation. Examples include encouraging peak performance from all employees, developing a flexible organization structure, managing service quality, implementing relationship banking, moving the bank to a sales culture, and managing change—to name a few. Recall that earlier in the book, it is skill in situations such as these that the best bank managers identified as the critical managerial challenges they face.

It is important to note that all of these situations really don't have much to do with banking. They have to do with managing. In addition, they are not problems in the medical sense, they are conditions. They are really a lot like allergies and psoriasis: they never go away. They cannot be cured or fixed and it is here that the effective bank manager behaves like a physician. The best bank managers solve (cure) the problems of banking and have learned to manage (treat) the conditions of banking.

The key of course is to know the difference. Physicians do but unfortunately many bankers do not. During the course of our research we ran across many bank managers who were doing something their doctor would never do. They were trying to "cure" conditions. We found:

- A CEO who tried to cure the condition of implementing a sales culture by dictating that everyone must begin selling.
- A senior officer who tried to cure the condition of strategic planning by purchasing all senior officers a copy of a particular business best seller.
- A retail banker who tried to cure the condition of implementing relationship banking by simply changing the title of installment lender to personal banker.
- A marketing director who tried to cure the condition of implementing a sales culture by issuing specific sales goals to contact personnel without a moment's training.
- A human resource director who tried to cure the condition of motivating peak performance by purchasing all branch managers a copy of a business best seller with a 60-second solution.
- Many CEOs and senior bankers who try to cure the condition of developing a high-performance culture with dinners, breakfasts, slogans, balloons, and lapel buttons, thus confusing leadership with promotion.

---

The best bank managers solve the problems of banking and manage the conditions of banking.

---

In each of these cases the managers believed they were being decisive, effective managers and that the action they took was all that was necessary to deal with the situation. Physicians know that trying to cure a condition is a waste of time and money. Doing the above and nothing more is wasting your time and the bank's money. Such activities are undoubtedly very useful but are not substitutes for leadership and management. The best bank managers know this. Like the physician, they separate the problems of the business from the conditions of the business.

Unfortunately, for most bank managers, the newest and most frustrating parts of their job are the conditions they must now manage. In many respects solving problems is much easier. They have solutions or at least specific endpoints where a decision must be made. Consequently, because many bankers are not used to managing conditions the natural tendency is to deal with them as if they were a problem. It is very tempting to try to apply a cure, a solution—often a quick fix. But strategic planning, managing change, peak performance, product management, relationship banking, sales management, service quality, and similar conditions cannot be cured or solved. They do not go away.

No, the best bank managers know that treating conditions requires management and leadership in the truest sense. They understand that the conditions they face require constant attention and fine-tuning and the realization that we will never return to the same situation we faced before. Skill in banking is as critical as ever but skill in managing is now more critical than ever.

## WHAT YOU DO IS AT LEAST AS IMPORTANT AS WHAT YOU PLAN TO DO

Earlier in the book we saw that the best bank managers somehow seem to know that while developing bank strategy is an outside → in process, the changes necessary to implement the strategy involve an inside → out process that begins with themselves.

---

When something goes wrong, less-effective bank managers often blame the strategy or the people who do the work.

---

Carrying this very important point further, it means that in order for a bank to achieve its objectives, it must not only *formulate* but also *implement* its strategies effectively. Success depends on a sound strategy and sound implementation. For example:

- A bank cannot effectively implement a relationship banking strategy without quality personnel and a supportive organization structure.

- A new-product development strategy cannot succeed without some mechanism in the bank to manage it.
- A bank cannot effectively implement a successful sales strategy without training, measurement, rewards, and full management support.

If either strategy development or implementation is done poorly, the result is likely to be failure of the overall strategy. The best bank managers are aware of and appreciate the important relationship between strategy and implementation. Unfortunately, this is not the case with less-effective bank managers. When a strategy fails they are often very quick to *blame the strategy* One CEO stated emphatically that "Sales will never work in banking." The head of retail banking in a large bank believes that "Relationship banking is good theory but cannot work in practice." Or they will *blame the people* who do the work. Several senior bankers in our study stated in one way or another, "Our people just refuse to sell." One CEO commented, "The people in our trust department will never be able to work with our retail people."

The relationship between strategy development and implementation is so critical that some people argue that it is impossible to determine whether a strategy is correct or not if the implementation is unsound. The relationship shown in Figure 3–1 presents the possible outcomes of four combinations of strategy development and implementation.[5]

*Success* is the most likely outcome when a bank has a good strategy and implements it well. In this case, all that can be done to ensure success *has* been done. It does not mean that success will follow because forces outside the bank's control, such as competitive moves, customer changes, or plain bad luck may still make a strategy unsuccessful. However, bank objectives have the best chance of being achieved when both strategy and implementation are done well. For example, a CEO whose strategy is to develop a true sales culture and seeks to implement it with proper employee selection, training, measurement, and rewards has done all that can be done to ensure success.

*Failure* is the most likely outcome to occur when a poorly

**FIGURE 3–1**
**The Relationship between Strategy Development and Implementation**

Strategy development

|  |  | Good | Poor |
|---|---|---|---|
| Strategy implementation | Good | Success | Roulette |
|  | Poor | Trouble | Failure |

*Reprinted with permission of The Free Press, a Division of Macmillan, Inc., from *The Marketing Edge: Making Strategies Work*, by Thomas V. Bonoma. Copyright © 1985 by The Free Press.

formulated strategy is poorly implemented. A bank with a poorly conceived and priced checking account package being sold by customer service representatives with no sales training, little desire to sell, and a bad opinion of the product will most certainly find itself in this cell. In these situations, management will have difficulty identifying the problem because poor strategy is masked by poor implementation. If the bank retains the same strategy and improves implementation all it will have gained is the ability to execute a poor strategy. If it reformulates its strategy and implements in the same manner, it will still fail. Obviously, a problem in this cell is difficult to diagnose because a poorly developed strategy has been poorly implemented. Thus, two things are wrong.

*Trouble* is the cell where we see the critical importance of implementation. In this situation, poor implementation sabotages a well-formulated strategy. The problem in many banks as we pointed out earlier is that the strategy often gets blamed (i.e., "sales won't work," "packaging of products cannot work in our market," "officer call programs are a waste of time.") Because many bankers are more accustomed to focusing on strategy formulation, the real problem—poor implementation—is often not diagnosed. When things go wrong, these bankers often call in the consultants and reformulate the strategy rather than question its implementation. The new (and often *less* appropriate) strategy is then reimplemented and continues to fail.

A senior retail banker recounted just such an experience in her bank. A senior citizens' package account was developed and launched with great expectations. After three months, results were dismal. Management believed that the product had been poorly priced. They repriced the product, and relaunched it with greater promotion. Results were worse this time. According to the retail banker the problem eventually was identified. The incentive program was viewed as unfair by those who were to sell the product, and problems existed in the amount of credit received for opening a new account versus converting an existing account. Consequently, those who were to implement the strategy saw little advantage in doing so. Unfortunately, management concentrated on strategy when the problem was implementation.

This situation is always particularly painful because managers can never objectively assess the adequacy of a strategy if they do not have the ability to implement the strategy. It is impossible to evaluate a strategy if we are incapable of implementing it effectively.

*Roulette* involves situations in which a poorly formulated strategy is implemented well. It is called roulette because it is impossible to predict the consequences in such a situation. Two basic outcomes may occur. The good implementation may overcome the poor strategy. Customer service reps may selectively "ignore" certain management directives that they know will not work, thereby forcing management to succeed in spite of themselves. They may also provide management an early warning of impending failure and give them time to correct any problems. Unfortunately, good implementation of a poor strategy can also hasten the failure of a poor strategy. This is why it is impossible to predict exactly what will happen in the roulette cell.

It should be clear that what the bank actually does is at least as important as what they plan to do. In other words, strategy implementation is at least as important as strategy development. Unfortunately, we found that less-effective bank managers are inclined simply to assume that effective implementation will occur and when it doesn't, they often abdicate their responsibility to manage and blame the strategy or people.

Finally, the quality of a strategy is difficult if not impossible to assess in the absence of effective implementation. Diagnosing why a strategy failed in the roulette, trouble and failure situations requires the analysis of *both* formulation and implementation. However, when in doubt look first to implementation problems and fix them. Then problems with strategy can be more clearly seen.

---

A strategic response to change requires a strategy.

---

## STRATEGIC RESPONSES TO CHANGE

We know that change is a constant in the new banking environment and that managing change is one of the critical management challenges identified in our research. The next two chapters present a strategy for systematically managing change. At this point, however, our final lesson in good management and leadership is the importance of a clearly defined strategy in dealing with threats and opportunities. There is a very important link between the existence of a clearly defined strategy and responding to change which can provide a real advantage to a bank manager.

The advantage is that they have a starting point when trying to assess the impact of an external change or when contemplating making an internal change. And that starting point is their strategy. Let us never forget that a strategic response to change requires a strategy.

One of the great benefits of having a clearly defined strategy is when your bank or unit must respond to change.[6] We already know that some change is external (technological, regulatory, economic, competition) and some change is internal (organization structure, new management, business philosophy). How well the bank or unit responds to change is key to its success and survival.

When facing an *external change* (threat or opportunity), the best bank managers begin with such questions as:

1. What does our strategy suggest how we should react to this change?
2. Does it suggest a reformulation, a modification, or an extension of our current strategy?
3. Does it suggest that we maintain the strategic status quo?

Constant reference to your strategy prevents knee-jerk responses to external change.

When facing an *internal change*, the best bank managers begin with such questions as:

1. Is this change in support of our strategy?
2. Does it suggest a reformulation, a modification, or an extension of our current strategy?
3. Is the proposed change worth it?

When a proposed internal change passes these questions, the discussion can then move to implementation concerns.

Having a clearly defined strategy enables a strategic response to change. What is the alternative response? If your bank or unit is facing external or internal change and you are unable to respond strategically by asking the above questions, then the direction of your bank or unit will be determined by whatever threat or opportunity you happen to be pursuing or avoiding at the particular moment. And that is simply not good management.

# PART 3

# MANAGING CHANGE

The art of progress is to preserve order amid change and to preserve change amid order.

*Alfred North Whitehead*

# CHAPTER 4

---

# STARTING RIGHT: IDENTIFYING AND DIAGNOSING THE NEED FOR CHANGE

---

*It appears to be a human tendency to seek solutions even before the problem is understood.*

N. R. F. Maier
T. R. Hoffman

Banks of all sizes and locations have been forced to deal with change for most of the last decade. In fact, bank CEOs and senior officers from across the country made it clear to us that the very survival of banks as institutions depends upon their ability to manage change effectively. Hardly a bank in the country is not now attempting in some way to manage change. Managing change is a skill that bank managers must acquire whether they are (1) merging two bank cultures, (2) reorganizing a single bank, (3) developing a sales orientation, (4) implementing a strategic planning process, (5) improving employee performance, or all of the above. It is not surprising therefore, that managing change was identified by CEOs and senior officers as one of the critical challenges bankers will face in the future. In our two-chapter sequence on managing change we will present a strategy for effectively managing change. We begin with two actual episodes.[1]

## Strategic Planning at Maxibank

A multibillion dollar bank affiliated with a holding company undertook a major strategic planning effort at the insistence of the recently appointed CEO. The strategic plan was to be the vehicle by which the bank would become a high-performance, market-driven organization with all its products and functions integrated to serve previously identified market segments.

With the active support and participation of the CEO, the process began with an announcement to all employees through the monthly newsletter and the appointment of a planning team to coordinate the process. The team included all the division managers and some key unit managers. The planning team developed a mission statement and objectives for the next five years, planned a work agenda of necessary tasks and due dates, and formed several task forces to do the analysis of key strategic issues.

The task forces included managerial and nonmanagerial personnel who were assigned specific issues to analyze. The issues included:

1. Internal strengths and weaknesses.
2. External threats and opportunities.
3. Retail market segments and needs.
4. Small business segments and needs.
5. Corporate segments and needs.
6. Agricultural segments and needs.

The planning team directed the task force to prepare written analyses of the issues and to make their reports within four weeks. After the initial identification of market needs, the reports of all six groups would be consolidated and the four market-issue task forces (numbers 3–6 above) would identify the strategy that the bank would develop to serve each market. The strategies would identify the product and service mix for each market and the responsibility of each division and unit. The various strategies were to be ready for presentation to the planning team three weeks later. The entire process was to be completed within eight weeks from the initial announcement to the final adoption of the strategic plan.

By any standard, the strategic planning was textbook perfect. It had all the ingredients of success: a participatory process to encourage a sense of ownership and a market-driven content to assure a responsive strategy as the outcome. But within a very short period of time it became apparent to the CEO that the task force groups were floundering. He began to hear reports that they were making very little progress and that a lot of time was being spent on issues having little to do with the strategic plan. When the four weeks passed and none of the groups had finished their analyses, the CEO was forced to confront the possibility that the strategic plan for the bank would not be done on time if at all. In fact, it was not completed, and the entire process was later abandoned.

What happened? Before thinking about this bank's apparent lack of success, let us describe another bank manager's experience with change.

### Developing a Performance Culture at First Community Bank

A considerably smaller bank undertook a major change in the way its branch managers performed their jobs. The CEO initiated the change because he had become increasingly unhappy with the bank's branch managers' lack of interest in doing anything other than making loans and administration. They seemed to have little interest in broader managerial issues affecting the bank. He noticed that whenever he held meetings with the entire group of branch managers, their informal conversations seldom focused on bank matters; rather they talked about sports, families, the weather, and the like. The CEO had no difficulty accepting the idea that employees have lives outside the bank. He did, however, believe that an effective bank was run by bank officers who not only performed their primary tasks competently, but also sought out opportunities to contribute to planning activities, problem solving, and other managerial tasks.

His objective was to find a way to motivate the branch managers to take an interest in being contributing members of the bank's management team. He decided to schedule monthly meetings with all the bank officers, including the branch managers, to discuss broad issues, such as the bank's overall goals, personnel policy, productivity, strategic issues, and compensation. The monthly meetings were disappointing and soon became little more than a forum for one-way communication from the CEO to those present at the meeting. The CEO decided to increase the frequency of the meetings and to ask for individual reports on how to deal with management problems and issues. But the results of this approach were even more disappointing because the quality of reports demonstrated clearly a lack of commitment. Apparently, the branch managers were not motivated, and the CEO could not understand why his efforts had failed. He believed he had made a clear attempt to apply the principles of participative management to enrich the job of branch manager thereby enabling them to be more valuable employees. All of the best-selling management books he had read in the past year had recommended the approach he took.

But what happened here? Both CEOs tried to initiate change in their banks. What do their change efforts have in common? How are they different? Why did they fall short of expectations? These are not easy questions to answer.

In too many instances, bank managers blame the change technique itself when results do not match expectations. For example, the CEOs who undertook the changes described above were convinced when the process was over that strategic planning and participative management *do not work*. In other instances, we heard the same thing about relationship banking ("It looks good on paper, but we tried it, and it doesn't work") and about officer call programs ("They don't work because people won't make their calls"). We also heard similar things about sales training, incentive programs, performance improvement, and quality improvement programs.

In other words, bankers tend to blame what they have done (the strategy, or technique) rather than how they went about doing it. The first comparison we will make between the two episodes is that the CEOs failed because of the way management implemented the change.

---

Every bank is an ongoing entity with a history and a culture that favors the continuation of existing behavior and activities.

---

How should they have implemented the changes? That question leads to the purpose of this chapter and the following one. There is only one way to maximize the probability that the change itself will be successful. Some important prerequisites are provided in Figure 4–1.[2] These two chapters will present

**FIGURE 4–1**
**The Prerequisites for an Effective Change Effort**

1. *It is planned and long term.* Successfully managing change involves all of the ingredients that go into managerial planning. It involves goal setting, action planning, implementation, monitoring, and taking corrective action when necessary. There is no such thing as a quick fix.

2. *It is problem oriented.* It identifies a specific problem in the bank and chooses an alternative solution which is then implemented to solve the problem.

3. *It reflects a systems approach.* The solution cannot be evaluated entirely in terms of its impact on the problem because it will have effects apart from the intended impact.

4. *It is action oriented.* Any change effort in your bank should focus on accomplishments and results. The emphasis is on getting things done which requires clear measurable impacts of what will be done.

5. *It requires a facilitator.* Successful change usually requires the facilitative role of a change agent to assist the bank.

6. *It involves learning principles.* Most change in your bank requires some reeducation. Successful reeducation requires the application of some basic learning principles.

the basic framework of a strategy for managing change in the banking industry.[3] Furthermore, we will analyze the reasons for failures of the two CEOs based on this framework.

## LEARNING PRINCIPLES INVOLVED IN MANAGING CHANGE

To really understand how changes are brought about in people, it is essential to understand some basic principles of learning. Many banks' efforts to change achieve very little because they overlooked the importance of providing reinforcement or continuous feedback to those who were being asked to change. These are basic principles of learning, and they must be incorporated into any change effort undertaken.

## Expectations and Motivations

People must want to learn. They may need more computer skills, sales skills, negotiating skills, or writing skills. They may need a better understanding of how the bank makes money and of what other units in the bank do. Some people recognize this need and are receptive to learning. Others reject it because to them, learning is an admission that their current level of job competence is inadequate. Both groups face the prospect of change with different expectations and motivations.

Determining other people's expectations and motivations is not an easy challenge, but one that must be done. Not everyone wants to participate in a change program—senior bankers as well as recent hires. Your job is to show them why they should want to change.

## Reinforcement and Feedback

An important principle of learning is reinforcement. This principle tells us that when people receive positive rewards, or feelings for doing something, it becomes more likely that they will do the same thing in the same or a similar situation. Or as one senior banker summarized it:

> What gets rewarded, gets done.

The other side of the coin tells us that negative reinforcement decreases the probability of doing the same thing at another time. The principle, then, implies that it would be easier to achieve successful change by using positive rewards.

The problem of course is the determination of reinforcers. That is, what will serve as the appropriate reinforcer of desired behavior? Money or praise may be for some people while others may be more responsive to time off or some type of educational experience. Obviously, situations and people determine which means of reinforcement proves effective. Employees generally desire to know how they are doing. This is especially true after a change has been implemented. Providing information about the progress of a unit allows employees to take corrective action.

Providing feedback long after an action has occurred is not as effective as providing feedback immediately after the action. As you might expect, individuals differ in their receptivity to feedback. In general, feedback is more favorably received by employees who are motivated to improve themselves or their unit of the bank.

## SUCCESSFULLY MANAGING CHANGE

A bank change effort may be one time or ongoing; it may attempt to improve the effectiveness of individuals, groups, or the entire bank. Whatever the focus, it is important to know that success will depend on understanding and applying three points:

1. Change involves reeducation, or relearning processes.
2. Banks are systems of interrelated parts. This simply means that any change will have effects apart from the intended impact and it is wise to anticipate these effects.
3. The success or failure of change depends upon both technique and implementation.

In each and every instance where we found a successful change, the bank manager understood and practiced these principles in one way or another.

---

There is only one way of managing change that maximizes the probability that the change itself will be successful.

---

Managing change involves a five-step sequence bank managers must take in the proper order. The five steps are actually a series of cause-effect relationships beginning with internal or external forces for change (the initial cause) and ending with the employees' acceptance of the change (the final effect).[4] They are shown in Figure 4–2. The first three steps focus on identifying and diagnosing the need for change, which is the subject of this chapter. The final two steps focus on implemen-

**FIGURE 4–2**
**Guidelines for Managing Change**

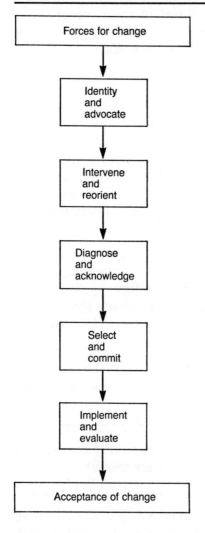

tation and overcoming resistance to change, which will be the subject of the next chapter.

## Step One: Identify and Advocate

The first step begins with the buildup of pressure to change that originates with either external or internal forces (or both) and ends with management's recognition that change is necessary. The most important effect of this first step is management's unequivocal advocacy of the necessity to undergo change. Management must support and defend the need for change or none will occur. The following statement from a CEO is clear in its support of the necessity for change·

> Initiating and adapting to change presents a tremendous challenge to me and to my senior people. But it is a necessity that we have to deal with and will deal with. I will not allow us to frustrate our outstanding younger officers.

Banks seldom undertake significant change without a strong shock from their environment. The industry has experienced shock forces to a degree unparalleled in its recent history. However, the effects of these environmental forces are unevenly experienced within the industry so that some bank managers can defer recognizing that they and their banks must change. Contrast the above statement with the following one made by another CEO:

> I am old-fashioned and believe the "note cage" is *the Bank*— was, is, will be. So has there really been much change in banking?

Other bank managers have not had the luxury of relative isolation and have no choice but to respond. The signals of external forces are: deteriorations of performance criteria (e.g., rates of return, interest margins, cost of funds and liquidity) and/or de clines in indicators of competitive strength (e.g., market share, volume of accounts, net acquisition of new accounts).

Internal forces for change occur *within* the bank and can usually be traced to process problems and people problems. The process problems include breakdowns in decision making and communications. Decisions are not being made, are made too late, or are of poor quality. The increase since deregulation in the volume of decisions alone led to this comment by a CEO:

> Before deregulation there weren't many decisions to make. Now I spend a lot of time building an organization structure that can deal with decision making on a timely basis.

Other indications of process problems are breakdowns in communications Communications are short-circuited, redundant, or simply inadequate. In many instances, tasks are not undertaken or not completed because the person responsible did not get the word. Finally, interpersonal conflicts, interdepartmental conflicts, and turf battles reflect breakdowns in processes.

Low levels of employee commitment and morale and high levels of absenteeism and turnover are symptoms of people problems. A certain level of employee discontent exists in most organizations, and banks are no exception, but in an environment where we must get better results from people, and fast, there is great danger if we ignore people problems.

The first step in successfully managing change is obviously the recognition that change is necessary. At this point, management must decide to act or not to act. Unfortunately, in many banks, the need for change goes unrecognized until some major catastrophe occurs. For example:

- Good customers move their business to competitors.
- Examiners draw attention to inadequate loan-loss provisions.
- Key officers resign.

Often these events occur before management fully recognizes the need for action.

Successful change efforts are directly related to the depth of top management's commitment and support of these efforts. Thus, it is absolutely imperative that top management recognize the signals and advocate the change process. This critical step also activates a powerful learning principle: Before people willingly relearn, they must first be convinced that what they now know is inadequate. Individuals must want to learn and that occurs most strongly when they recognize that they are unable to cope effectively in their present jobs using their existing knowledge and behavior. The following statement from a senior banker is very clear in its recognition of the need for change:

> About three years ago I was forced to recognize that my job had outgrown my skills as a manager and that I had to do something about it.

---

**Analysis and Insight**

Both Maxibank and Community Bank went through this first step. In both cases, top management recognized and advocated the need for change. The CEO of Maxibank identified external factors as the force creating the pressure to change. The CEO of Community Bank responded to internal forces. Both CEOs were active advocates for change, and they took personal charge of the change strategy.

---

## Step Two: Intervene and Reorient

Step two is an application of the idea that every bank is an ongoing entity with a history and a culture that favor the continuation of existing behaviors and activities. As one senior banker put it:

> Banks have evolved into creatures of routine and repetition. And change hurts. So it's not surprising that we often hear the cry to "get back to basics." I don't know what that means. I think it means, "I wish we could put everything back the way it was."

In order to change the present system, it is necessary to intervene and reorient it to accept the need to change.

---

Before people willingly relearn, they must first be convinced that what they now know is inadequate.

---

People tend to seek answers in traditional solutions. Thus, when bank managers become advocates of change, the danger exists that they will also become advocates for using solutions that they have previously implemented. For this reason it may be necessary to bring in an outsider if the managers are unable to be facilitators of change as well as champions of change. Change agents or facilitators bring different perspectives to the situation and serve as challengers to the status quo. The success of any bank change program rests heavily on the quality and workability of the relationship between those implementing change and the key personnel in the bank. Thus, how management intervenes is a crucial phase of step two. There are three basic forms of intervention that bankers can use.

### Forms of Intervention

*External Facilitators.*   External change agents are actually temporary employees of the bank since they are hired only for the duration of the change process whether it be the implementation of a sales management structure or to facilitate a merger. They originate in a variety of organizations including consulting firms, training organizations, and universities. It is critical, however, that they are familiar with bank culture and practice and have training in management and change processes. Only with this kind of training will the external change agent have the perspective to facilitate the change process in a bank.

*Internal Facilitators.*   The internal agent of change is an employee of the bank. We have found that this individual is often a recently appointed CEO or senior officer of an institution that has a record of poor performance, and the individual took the job with the expectation that major change was necessary.

*External-Internal Change Teams.*   Some banks have successfully used an external-internal change team to intervene and develop programs. In fact, many change consultants demand an internal team. This approach attempts to use the resources and knowledge of both external and internal people and usually designates one individual or small group within the bank to work with the external team as spearheads of the change effort. The internal group will often come from the human resources department, but we have also seen it be a group of top managers

*Analysis and Insight*

It is clear that the CEO of Maxibank was an internal change agent brought in to intervene and reorient the bank. The CEO of Community Bank was also an internal change agent. Unfortunately he had no apparent mandate to change. At Maxibank, the CEO attempted to be both the advocate of change and the facilitator of change. The CEO of Community Bank advocated change, but had difficulty being the facilitator. The more fundamental the change, the more an external change agent is needed, and the CEO of Community Bank was attempting to make one of the most difficult changes of all; a fundamental change in the way people behave.

Maxibank's CEO was also attempting fundamental change: There is probably no change more fundamental than that brought about by strategic analyses and planning. Perhaps he also attempted to play too large a role, and an external facilitator or an external-internal team approach would have enabled him to avoid some of the problems that led to the eventual failure of the change effort.

## Approaches to Facilitate Intervention

Whether internal or external to the bank, the person or group selected to facilitate can relate to the bank according to one of four approaches.[5]

*The Medical Approach.* Perhaps the most basic of all approaches, the medical approach places the facilitator in the role of advisor. Management asks the individual or team to assist in clarifying the problems, diagnosing the causes, and recommending courses of action, but retains the responsibility for accepting or rejecting any recommendations. The relationship is much like that of the physician-consultant arrangement; that is, the physician may seek opinions from other experts, but the choice of therapy remains with the physician.

*The Doctor-Patient Approach.* Here the bank is the "patient" who suspects that something is wrong. The change agent—the doctor—diagnoses and prescribes a solution that, of course, can be rejected by the patient. Yet by virtue of the relationship, the bank usually adopts the recommendations. The facilitator does the diagnosis and problem-identification activities jointly with the organization. The more involved the bank is in the process, the more likely management is to accept the recommended solution.

*The Engineering Approach.*    This approach can be used when the bank has performed the diagnostic work and has decided on a specific solution. For example, several banks in our study had decided after varying periods of study that a reorganization was necessary. They then sought the aid of experts to aid in implementing the reorganization.

*The Process Approach.*    This approach is widely used by some consultants and involves an actual collaboration of the bank and the change agents through which management is encouraged to see and understand the bank's problems. Through joint efforts, managers and change agents try to comprehend the factors in the situation that must be changed to improve performance  The facilitator avoids taking sole responsibility for either diagnosis or prescription; rather, the emphasis is on enabling management to comprehend the problems. The emphasis is on teaching management *how* to diagnose rather than on doing the diagnosing for management. The first three approaches are much more widely used in banking than this approach.

Where the facilitator of change comes from and the approach used are very important issues which must be decided before any change effort is undertaken. We have not seen a change effort of any magnitude succeed without first having these two issues decided. It is not a question of one approach being superior. It will depend on the characteristics of the facilitator, the bank, and the situation. What is critical is to make a choice prior to initiating any change effort, and stick with it.

The desired outcome in step two is to reorient the bank's employees toward alternative solutions. The achievement of this outcome should dictate which approach is used. Only when employees are sufficiently ready to learn new ways of doing things should the third step be undertaken.

### Step Three: Diagnose and Acknowledge the Problem

This step involves diagnosing all the symptoms of a problem so that all the people who must implement any possible solutions acknowledge that the problem in fact exists. It is not enough for management to acknowledge the problem unless they alone are the ones to solve it. This step when properly implemented deepens the commitment to change by presenting concrete evidence that the status quo is unacceptable.

Management must support and defend the need for change or none will occur.

Effective diagnosis of the problem must obviously precede any action. Experience and judgment are critical to this step unless the problem is readily apparent. Ordinarily, however, bank managers will disagree on the nature of the problem depending on where they view it from. There is no formula for accurate diagnosis, but the following questions point in the right direction.

1  What is the problem as distinct from the symptoms of the problem?
2. What must be changed to solve the problem?
3. What outcomes (objectives) are expected from the change, and how will those outcomes be measured?

The task of problem identification is greatly facilitated when managers view the bank as a system of interrelated elements as we stated at the opening of the chapter. This idea, illustrated in Figure 4–3, compares the bank to an iceberg. This analogy draws attention to two important elements: the *formal* and *informal* components. The formal components are that part

**FIGURE 4–3**
**The Bank as an Iceberg**

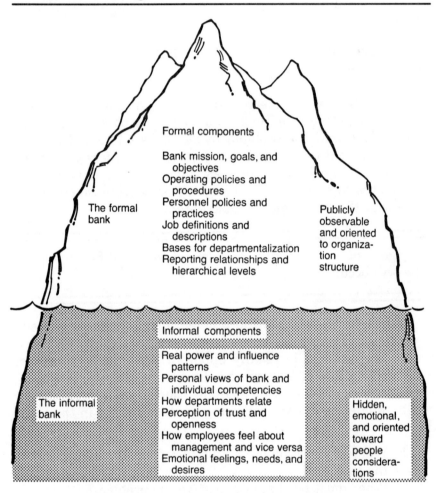

Formal components

Bank mission, goals, and
    objectives
Operating policies and
    procedures
Personnel policies and
    practices
Job definitions and
    descriptions
Bases for departmentalization
Reporting relationships and
    hierarchical levels

The formal
bank

Publicly
observable
and oriented
to organiza-
tion
structure

Informal components

Real power and influence
    patterns
Personal views of bank and
    individual competencies
How departments relate
Perception of trust and
    openness
How employees feel about
    management and vice versa
Emotional feelings, needs, and
    desires

The informal
bank

Hidden,
emotional,
and oriented
toward
people
considera-
tions

of an iceberg that is "above water"; the informal components lie
below water, unseen, but there nevertheless.[6]

As the iceberg indicates, the formal components are observable, rational, and related to the organization structure of
the bank. The informal components are, on the other hand, not
observable to all people, often irrational, and oriented to pro-

cess and people factors. Like an iceberg, a bank is an integrated whole, and changes in any one part will change the nature of the whole.

At one extreme are problems that lie with the structure of the bank. Management can solve these problems by changing job descriptions, departmentalization bases, and reporting relationships, or as in many banks by a total reorganization. At the other extreme are problems which lie with the way people behave toward each other and other departments. Generally speaking, the greater the scope and intensity of the problem, the more likely it is that the problem will be found in the informal components. These problems are related to personal views, value orientations, feelings, and sentiments for both individuals as well as departments. While these factors can certainly be affected by changing the bank's organization structure, they are deep seated, and management must confront them more directly.

Diagnosing problems requires collecting information. Several sources include:

1. Opinions of employees.
2. Direct observations of actual behavior in the workplace.
3. Interviews with selected officers in key positions.
4. Interviews with groups of employees to explore different views of the same problem.
5. Examination of documents and records for historical and current information.

Regardless of how the information is collected, the important concern is that it be presented in forums where all who are involved can evaluate the evidence. The desired outcome of step three is widespread acknowledgment that the problem has been properly identified, whether in the formal or informal components of the bank. Only then should managers move to the fourth step which begins the process of implementation of the solution. Steps four and five of our guidelines for managing change focus on implementation and are covered in the next chapter.

### Analysis and Insight

Clearly the CEOs of Maxibank and Community Bank skipped this step. However they went about diagnosing, they certainly did not involve their people in the process. They announced the solutions—strategic analysis and enrichment of jobs—without involving the people who were going to have to implement the solutions. No doubt the CEOs had their reasons for believing that their solutions were appropriate solutions. For that matter, they may very well have been appropriate solutions. But whether the solutions are appropriate becomes irrelevant when the people who must implement them reject them.

Exactly where in the iceberg these two CEOs believed the problems to lie is anybody's guess. As we will see in the next chapter, strategic analysis and job enrichment are quite different techniques and are appropriate responses to problems at different levels in the iceberg.

# CHAPTER 5

---

# ORCHESTRATING THE FUTURE: IMPLEMENTING CHANGE AND OVERCOMING RESISTANCE TO CHANGE

---

*Nothing endures but change.*

Heraclitus

Because change is a permanent feature of the banking industry, skills in identifying and diagnosing the need for change are critical. However, these skills are necessary but not sufficient for effectively managing change. Sooner or later, change must be implemented and any resistance to change must be overcome. These two final steps of our five guidelines for managing change are the subject of this chapter.

---

When there is a large discrepancy between culture and change, it is likely that culture will win and change will lose.

---

## PREPARING TO IMPLEMENT CHANGE

It is now time to select the specific action to facilitate the change process. The choice of a particular technique depends on the nature of the problem that management has diagnosed. Management must determine which alternative is most likely to produce the desired outcome, whether it is improvement in the skills, attitudes, and behavior of employees or in the bank's organization structure. As noted in Chapter 4, diagnosing the problem includes specifying the outcome that management desires from the change. Before moving to step four, which begins the implementation process, prepare yourself by (1) assessing the climate for change, and (2) selecting a strategy for implementation.

## The Climate for Change

There are three factors that will influence the outcome of any change effort in your bank, and they must be acknowledged prior to any attempt at change.

   **1.** *The leadership climate in the bank.*   Every bank has a work environment or climate that results from the leadership style and administrative practices of management. Any change, no matter the magnitude, that does not have the support and commitment of management has only a slim chance of success. Attempts at developing a sales culture fail many times when management assumes it is for everyone in the bank except them. Everything else in the process may be done correctly but the critical ingredient is missing. The most effective bank managers understand that change is a process beginning with themselves.

   **2.** *The formal bank organization.*   The proposed change must be compatible with those elements at the top of the iceberg and include management philosophy, policies, systems of control, and the organization structure. Of course, some of these factors may be the target of the change effort. The important point is that a change in one factor must be compatible with all the others. Trying to implement a product management system or a true sales management system will almost certainly fail if the bank's organization structure remains one based on banking functions. Such strategies are not compatible with a functional organization structure. Trying to implement an incentive compensation system in only one part of the bank will have effects outside that area and they will usually be negative ones.

   **3.** *The bank's culture.*   Probably the best definition of the abstract concept of organizational culture was provided by a senior banker:

It's the way we do things around here.

Culture is the web of values, shared beliefs, assumptions, and behaviors that employees of a bank acquire over time. In many ways it is similar to an individual's personality. It is the traditional way that people have always behaved at work. Any attempt at change that runs counter to the expectations and attitudes of groups in the bank is likely to be resisted. When there is a large discrepancy between culture and change, it is likely that culture will win and change will lose.

Implementation of change that does not consider the limits imposed by the prevailing leadership climate, formal organization, and the bank's culture may amplify the problem that triggered the need for change in the first place. In addition, the potential for subsequent problems is greater. Taken together, the prevailing conditions constitute the climate for change, and they can be positive or negative.

## Strategy for Implementation

Selecting a strategy for implementing change will have consequences in the final outcome. There are three basic approaches, located along a continuum, with unilateral authority at one extreme and delegated authority at the other extreme. In the middle of the continuum is shared authority.[1]

*Unilateral approaches* can take the form of a directive describing the change, and the responsibilities of subordinates in implementing it. We have seen instances where directives were sent announcing compulsory sales training and measurement of sales performance for all platform personnel, announcements of key personnel changes, and several instances where entire reorganizations were directed. One CEO announced that henceforth all employees should begin selling—and did nothing more.

*Shared approaches* involve lower-level groups in the process of either (1) defining the problem and alternative solutions, or (2) defining solutions only after higher-level management has defined the problem. In either case, the process utilizes the talents and insights of all members at all levels.

Finally, *delegated approaches* give authority to the subordinate group affected. The group is ultimately responsible for the analysis of the problem as well as proposed solutions.

The more successful instances of change in banks of all sizes are those that tend toward the shared position on the continuum. This holds true for changes ranging from the design of jobs, quality improvement programs, or the implementation of a sales culture, to entire reorganizations of individual banks and mergers of different bank cultures.

The shared approach to implementing change is very popular and involves the joint efforts of both superiors and subordinates in the entire process. It undoubtedly appeals to our sense of democracy and fairness. But we have also seen this strategy fail in many instances. There is no guarantee that it will work in all cases. In fact, before employees participate in any change effort, consider these four questions:

**1.** *Do the employees want to become involved?*   We have seen situations where, for any number of reasons, they rejected the invitation. They may have more pressing demands, such as doing their own work. Unfortunately, in many instances the employees viewed the invitation to participate as a subtle (but not too subtle) attempt by management to manipulate them toward a solution already predetermined. Trust is a critical element for effective management. Employees will cynically resist attempts to involve them if the leadership climate or the bank culture has created an atmosphere of mistrust and insincerity.

**2.** *Are employees willing and able to voice their ideas?* Even if they are willing, employees must have the expertise in some aspect of the analysis. The technical problems associated with computer installation or automated processes may be beyond the training of tellers, yet they may have very valuable insights into the impact the change will have on their own jobs and on the customer.

**3.** *Are managers secure in their own positions?*   Insecure managers will almost surely perceive any participation by employees as a threat to their authority. They might view employee participation as a sign of weakness or as undermining their status. They must be secure enough to give credit for good ideas and to give explanations for ideas of questionable merit. In other words, the managers' personalities and leadership styles must be compatible with the shared approach to implementing change if it is to be successful. In the language of our peak performance chapter, a manager comfortable with the low-discretion model would not likely be comfortable with the shared approach to change. One CEO stated the problem another way:

> I believe that in our bank, the people at the top know what needs to be done. And the people at the bottom know what needs to be done. It's the people in the middle that are holding us back.

**4.** *Are managers open-minded to employees' suggestions?* If managers have predetermined the solution, the participation of employees will soon be recognized for what it is. Obviously management has final responsibility for the outcome and should control the situation by specifying beforehand what latitude will be given to employees: They may define objectives, establish constraints, or whatever, so long as bank employees know the rules prior to their participation.

If the answer to any of these questions is a definite no, then there will be a limit on effective participation. In this situation, the use of the shared approach (and delegated approach as well) should be viewed with caution. Leadership style, formal organization, bank culture, and characteristics of the employees are key factors constraining the entire change process.

Finally, the nature of the problem itself affects the choice of implementation strategy. If the problem requires immediate action, a unilateral approach may be the only means, since the other approaches take time.

---

If the leadership climate or the bank culture has created an atmosphere of mistrust and insincerity, most attempts to involve employees will be viewed by them in cynical terms and most likely will be resisted.

---

## Step Four: Select and Commit to a Solution

This step involves selecting the solution based on the diagnosed problem and obtaining the commitment of those who must implement it. The problem (e.g., sales capabilities of loan officers, inability to respond quickly with new products, quality of service), becomes the *target of change*, and it may be an element lying above or below the waterline of the bank iceberg. The solution (e.g., sales management system, new-product development process, quality improvement program) is a management technique or strategy that brings about the desired change in the target.

At this point you should determine how deep you must go into the iceberg to solve the problem. Figure 5–1 presents a way to accomplish this task. It suggests that there will usually be eight levels, or targets of change.[2] As the target moves from left to right, the deeper in the bank iceberg it will be and the more the solution will rely on changing people and less on organizational systems and technical expertise.

*Levels 1 through 4.* This group involves formal components including jobs, responsibilities and bases for departmentalization, policies, and practices. However, within this group the depth of change can vary from changing individual jobs to changing the entire structure of the bank. These targets of change are at a relatively low depth and involve relatively insensitive issues, which probably explains their popularity in banking.

*Levels 5 through 8.* Changes in this group target the informal components of the bank. Individual and group behavior, expectations, attitudes, and sentiments, are targets for change. Banks attempting to change their culture must obviously target these levels. Attempts by banks to become sales cultures or to break down the "Chinese Wall" that often exists between the traditional banking functions, involve changes deep in the iceberg. They involve changes in the behavior of individuals and groups. Although many public and private organizations have had great success in accomplishing change at levels 5 through 8, only a limited number of banks have done so successfully.

**FIGURE 5–1**
**Eight Targets of Change Efforts**

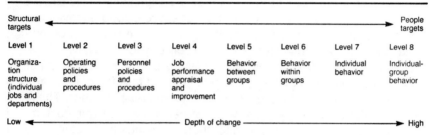

| Structural targets ← | | | | | | | People targets |
|---|---|---|---|---|---|---|---|
| Level 1 | Level 2 | Level 3 | Level 4 | Level 5 | Level 6 | Level 7 | Level 8 |
| Organization structure (individual jobs and departments) | Operating policies and procedures | Personnel policies and procedures | Job performance appraisal and improvement | Behavior between groups | Behavior within groups | Individual behavior | Individual-group behavior |

Low ←———————— Depth of change ————————→ High

*Multilevel changes.* More often than not the solution to significant bank problems will involve changes at more than one level. For example, leadership development and management by objectives have been used in combination with considerable success, when the problem involves inadequate merit-related performance evaluation practices. Some change techniques are inherently multilevel because of their profound effects. Strategic planning if implemented properly involves the bank at every level, from individual jobs to relationships among individuals and groups.

A successful change effort will complete step four with the assurance that key bank personnel have committed to the technique as the solution to the diagnosed problem. Whether that commitment exists depends on how the technique was selected. If the process to this point has caused the people who must implement the solution to confront the fact that the present system is personally and organizationally unrewarding, and if top management has steadfastly advocated the need for change, then the likelihood of success is high. Now let's return to our two change episodes.

---

*Analysis and Insight*

As we examine how the CEOs of Maxibank and Community Bank selected the techniques of strategic planning and job enrichment as solutions to their banks' problems, the apparent absence of commitment is understandable. In both banks, the CEO identified the problem and imposed the solution.

Maxibank's strategic analysis began to crack in the task forces when individuals from different divisions and units began to quarrel over matters having little to do with their assignments. This conflict demonstrated problems deep in the iceberg related to behavior between groups. Recall that these task forces were made up of individuals from units across the bank. Their day-to-day activities encouraged them to compete with individuals in other units, rather than to cooperate with them. The retail market task force, for example, included people from private banking and trust divisions. These two divisions had a long history of competing for the same customers, and there was no incentive for them to change that history. The problem had not been diagnosed in terms of conflicts between departments and the solution (strategic planning) had not provided for team building as a strategic analysis activity.

The lack of success at Community Bank can be traced to the CEO's failure to obtain commitment. The CEO stated that the branch managers were not motivated and he believed he could motivate them by enriching their jobs. What he failed to understand is that all behavior is motivated, and what he should have understood is that the branch managers were motivated to behave in ways that were contrary to effective bank performance. As soon as the problem is framed in these terms, it is apparent that individuals will continue their behavior until they have a reason to change. They, and they alone, determine what that reason or incentive must be. They were never given that opportunity and that was reason enough for their rejection of the CEO's solution.

## Step Five: Implement and Evaluate the Solution

The purpose of the final step is to implement and evaluate the solution on a small scale so as to identify any defects prior to imposing it throughout the bank. If the initial, modest attempts are successful, the commitment of people is reinforced by positive results. As management learns from each successive implementation, the total effort is strengthened. Not even the most detailed implementation plan can anticipate all the consequences of implementing a particular solution. Thus, it is necessary to search for new information that can improve the chances of success when the solution is implemented on a larger scale. Figure 5–2 provides some key issues to examine when evaluating a change effort.[3]

Management should also pay attention to selecting the appropriate time to implement the solutions. The matter of timing depends on a number of factors, particularly the bank's operating cycle. Certainly, if the solution is of considerable magnitude, it should not compete with day-to-day operations; thus, the change might well be implemented during a slack period. On the other hand, if the solution is vital to the survival of the bank, immediate implementation is necessary.

It is important to reemphasize that management cannot evaluate the effectiveness of change unless they established concrete, specific objectives during step four. A change that is undertaken to "make the bank a better place to work," or to "improve service quality," or to "develop the selling capabilities of the employees" cannot be evaluated. Measurable criteria

**FIGURE 5–2**
**Issues to Consider in Evaluating Change Efforts**

| Relevant Issues to Evaluate | What to Look for | Where to Look |
|---|---|---|
| 1. Have the employees learned, changed attitudes, and/or improved skills? | Attitudes and/or skills of employees before and after the change. | Comments of employees, co-workers, and superiors. |
| 2. Are change materials being used on the job? | The on-the-job performance and behavior of employees. | Attitudes as well as performance of employees. |
| 3. What are the costs of the change program? | The fixed and variable costs of the change. | Costs of consultants, employee time away from work, training expenses, travel expenses, and fixed costs. |
| 4. How long does the change program have an effect on employees? | The on-the-job performance and behavior of employees over an extended period of time. | Attitudes as well as performance of employees. |

that are valid indicators of the objectives must be developed. Otherwise you will have no bases for evaluation.

Positive indications that change is proceeding as planned reinforces the commitment of people to unlearn and relearn new ways of doing their job. Acceptance of the change is facilitated by its positive results.

---

### Analysis and Insight

Obviously neither Maxibank or Community Bank properly performed the last step. Both CEOs implemented the change on the largest possible scale. But the failure at step five does not account for the failure of the attempts at change. They were both doomed from the beginning. Maxibank's failure began at step two when the CEO unilaterally defined the problem. Community Bank's failure began at step one when the CEO attempted to be both advocate and facilitator of change, but mistakes are also seen at nearly every subsequent step.

---

## A GUIDE TO MANAGING CHANGE

The process of managing change in your bank must be approached systematically. The five-step strategy provides a systematic approach that increases the odds that the change will be successful. Of course, there are no guarantees. Banking is highly complex as are the individual banks that make up the industry. Appropriate responses to threats and opportunities are more likely to follow when the approach to change is systematic.

A history of having tried and failed hurts any future attempts to change, no matter how well intentioned or well managed.

Whether a bank is large or small, retail-oriented or corporate-oriented, money center or community, its managers can manage change effectively. They can use the five-step strategy to guide the actions they need to take as shown in Figure 5–3.[4]

Change creates new situations. These new situations are then sources or forces for change as problems and issues emerge. New settings become sources of problems and new tar

**FIGURE 5–3**
**Guidelines for Managing Change**

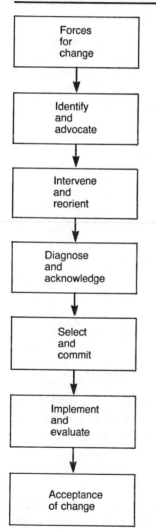

- Beginning with step one, identify as exactly as possible the forces for change and the reasoning behind your decision to advocate the necessity for change. Keep in mind that it is the depth and sincerity of commitment that is the issue here. If you are not convinced that change is necessary, no one else will be convinced.

- Step two's purpose is to reorient the bank to consider the entire range of possible actions. Confront honestly the issue of whether you can be both the advocate and the facilitator. Generally, the most recently appointed/hired manager has a better chance than one who has been on the job for awhile. The identification of the facilitator (change agent) then becomes critical.

- Step three has the dual purpose of accurate diagnosis and widespread acknowledgment of the problem. The manager and/or change agent must undertake actions that achieve both purposes. How you accumulate, analyze, and present information are more important determinants of whether the two purposes are achieved than what the information indicates.

- Step four provides a solution to the acknowledged problem and a commitment to make that solution work. Of the two, the latter is the more important. A partial solution with strong commitment will be more effective than a strong solution with weak commitment. There presently exists no more powerful technique than strategic analysis, but weak commitment can consign it to the scrap heap.

- Step five calls for implementing and evaluating the solution on a small scale. The whole idea is to get information that reinforces the validity of the solution as an effective response. As step five proceeds and as positive information is made public, the required new learning is reinforced. The solution can be phased into the entire bank level by level, unit by unit.

gets of change. The five-step strategy suggests no final solution; rather it emphasizes that a bank manager operates in a world wherein the only certainty is change itself.

To those bank managers who respond that they do not have time to go through each of the five steps in the manner described in these two chapters, they might remember a television commercial aired by a manufacturer of automobile filters. In the commercial, the mechanic warns the viewers that if they don't want to pay him now to install the filter, they can "pay me later" when the engine must be overhauled.

During the research for this book, we met many bank managers who have paid later for the time they saved by ignoring the importance of managing change. The most significant cost is the failure itself. Also, a history of having tried and failed hurts any future attempts to change, no matter how well intentioned or well managed.

## RESISTANCE TO CHANGE

Most bank change efforts eventually run into some form of employee resistance. Change triggers rational and irrational emotional reaction because of the uncertainty involved. Instead of assuming that employees will resist change or act in a particular manner, it is better to understand the reasons why people resist change.[5] There are four common reasons for resistance to change.

**1.** *Self-interest.* People will resist change because they fear the loss of something they value. Whether the change only involves additional training or whether it is a total reorganization of the bank, some people will fear loss of power, freedom to make decisions, control over resources, friendships, and prestige. When we fear loss, we think of ourselves and what we may have to give up. Remember that a fearful person has only his or her self-interest in mind when resisting change. The interests of the bank and of co-workers are not given much priority.

**2.** *Lack of trust.* Once again the mistrust of management appears as a barrier to effective bank management in the deregulated environment. It is almost a certainty that when people do not fully understand why change is occurring and what its implications are, they will resist it.

In banks where there is a great deal of mistrust of management, it is very likely that misunderstandings will occur when change is proposed. This mistrust is often based on other factors developed over the years and as we have seen in many banks, is well earned by management. One senior banker admitted:

> For years we didn't want employees to know how we made money. The goal was to keep the employees in the dark for as long as we could.

Secrecy at the top of many banks has done little to nurture trust in management. Hence, employees cynically look on the change effort as just another management ploy. The sentiments of employees are "Sales (or productivity, or whatever) is hot now. So let's just live through it."

**3.** *Different assessments.* Because bank employees will view change—its intent, potential consequences, and impact on them—differently, there are often different assessments of the situation. Those initiating the change see more positive results because of the change, while those being affected and not initiating the changes see more costs involved with the change. For example, the classic operations and customer-service struggle is usually the result of contradictory assessments rather than personality clashes among the groups' leaders and should be viewed as such.

Most bank cultures are in reality a collection of subcultures or "clans" that have developed over many years and are influenced heavily by the way most banks have been traditionally organized. Clearly, there are distinct cultural differences between the subcultures of data processing/operations, commercial lending, trust, retail, and investment banking. Thus, changes in technology or new management methods designed to increase productivity will have little success without concurrent changes in the beliefs and behaviors of other managers.

The problem is that managers who are attempting change often make two overly broad assumptions: (1) They have all the relevant data and information available to diagnose the situation, and (2) the people to be affected by the change also have the same facts. Whatever the circumstances, the initiators and those affected often have different data and information. This results in resistance to change. However, in some cases the resistance can be healthy for the bank, especially where the affected unit or department possess more valid data and information.

4. *Low tolerance for change.*  Bankers who have tried to build a sales orientation know that people often resist change when that change requires the development of new skills. People may understand clearly that change is necessary, but are emotionally unable to make the transition. A low tolerance for change also is found in banks among managers who resist change to save face. Many managers assume that making the necessary adjustments and changes is admitting that their previous behavior, decisions, and beliefs were wrong.

## Minimizing Resistance to Change

Successfully managing change in your bank involves recognizing that resisting change is a natural human response, and that steps must be taken to minimize resistance. Minimizing resistance can reduce the time it takes for a change to be accepted or tolerated. Otherwise, a poorly implemented change will result in no change, superficial change, short-term change, or distorted change.

A number of methods have proven useful in minimizing resistance to change which can be used in different situations and in various combinations.[6]

1. *Education and communication.*  A very good way to minimize resistance to change is to deal with it before it occurs. Communication and education help people prepare for the change. Paving the way, showing the necessity and logic for the change, and keeping everyone informed along the way will almost certainly cut down on resistance.

2. *Participation and involvement.*  Having the people who will be affected by the change help to design and implement it helps to increase their commitment to the change. If people feel

their ideas and attitudes are being included in the change effort, they will usually become less resistant and more receptive.

**3.** *Facilitation and support.* Being supportive when change is being implemented is critical. It is especially important for managers to be supportive (e.g., showing concern for subordinates, being a good listener, going to bat for subordinates on an issue that is important), and help facilitate the change when fear and anxiety are at the heart of the resistance.

**4.** *Negotiation and agreement.* Reducing resistance can often be brought about through negotiation. Discussion and analysis can often help managers from different functional departments in the bank identify points of negotiation and agreement.

**5.** *Explicit and implicit coercion.* Employees can always be coerced into going along with change by threatening them with job loss, reduced promotion opportunities, poor job assignments, and loss of privileges. Clearly such behavior is risky and increases the likelihood of greater problems down the road and increasing mistrust of management.

**6.** *Manipulation and co-optation.* Employees can be manipulated by holding back information, playing one department against another, and by providing slanted information. People can be co-opted by giving them a major and visible role in the design and implementation of the change. These methods are also very risky and have a high probability of backfiring in the long run.

# PART 4

# DEVELOPING RESPONSIVE ORGANIZATION STRUCTURES

For any one organization, the problem is to ensure that technology, structure, and goals are in harmony  That is what good management is all about

*Charles Perrow*

# CHAPTER 6

## GETTING IN YOUR OWN WAY: PROBLEMS IN ORGANIZATION STRUCTURE

*We have met the enemy and he is us.*
*Walt Kelly*

"The units in my bank behave more like competitors than part of the organization." Ask any room full of senior bankers if this statement applies to their bank and the first response is a roar of laughter and nods of agreement. But then the laughter usually quiets very quickly and sheepish looks appear on several faces as they begin looking around the room. Apparently what is funny for banks in general is not humorous when we realize it also applies to our bank. Somehow they know that things are not really supposed to be that way in well-managed, high-performance organizations.

Because of the importance of organization structure to effective bank performance, this two-chapter sequence focuses on this critical topic. This chapter concentrates on identifying problems in organization structure. The next chapter focuses on integrating bank structure and strategy.

The book's first chapter states that the factors holding back many banks have little to do with banking capability and everything to do with managing capability. Nowhere can this be illustrated any better than in the area of bank organization structure. Consider the following incidents.

### That's Not My Job

A large bank had several years previously initiated a "Women's Bank" as part of its retail bank. It was targeted primarily at professionals, executives, and entrepreneurs, and management was very pleased with its performance.

One morning, one of their best customers came in to borrow $15,000, fully secured by certificates of deposit in the bank. Unfortunately, the officer she had customarily dealt with was out of the bank for several days. Rather than ask her to come back when her boss was in or refer her to someone else, the secretary decided to help the customer with the details on the loan application.

Unfortunately, it became apparent that the details of the procedure were beyond the knowledge of the secretary. She excused herself and took the application to the private banking department. She explained to a private banker that one of their best customers was downstairs and that she was having problems serving the customer while her boss was out of town. She asked for his assistance to which he replied, "I'll only help with the application if she moves her account to the private banking department."

### What's in It for Me?

A regional bank made a commitment to implement a new strategy involving commission sales and incentive compensation for officers calling on middle-market businesses. The bank recruited several new officers in addition to some of their own best people. The entire group was given sales training by one of the nation's most successful industrial firms.

A few months into the new strategy, a young calling officer was told by a prospect that he would be able to consolidate a significant amount of deposits from several banks and place them in the officer's bank if a discount could be secured on a loan. On returning to his bank, the officer discussed the proposal with the individual in charge of commercial loans. His response to the proposal was, "What's in it for me?"

### How to Make a Strategic Decision

A small bank CEO decided that it was time for the bank to add a credit card. For several months the operations area and the lending area competed to be the department in which the card would be housed. The discussions became very heated on several occasions. After several months of continued debate, the CEO made his decision. Each department was allowed to have its own credit card.

Each of these incidents is true. Each illustrates the impact of organization structure on the behavior and performance of bank employees, and ultimately on bank performance.[1] They illustrate a very important truth for bank managers; *the biggest influence on how we behave at work, and what we think is important, is how the work is structured.* Each also illustrates the far too common organization structure problems that exist in many banks.

---

One of the most important principles of management is that strategy should dictate structure.

---

## THE IMPACT OF ORGANIZATION STRUCTURE

The contribution of organization structure to the performance of a bank is demonstrated every time an employee satisfies a customer's financial needs, makes a profitable loan, develops a new product, or devises a productivity improvement program. When employees do not do these things well, the chances are that the fault can be found in the organization structure. An effective organization structure is part of a high-performance bank because it enables qualified people to do their best work. A senior banker put it another way:

> While I have the freedom to hire and fire people, I found out it's more effective to change the way people do their job. Our reorganization efforts were aimed at changing the way jobs should be performed and thereby changing the way the people perform.

What we must realize is that different organization structures facilitate the accomplishment of different strategies in relation to the environment that the bank faces. A bank's organization structure must be consistent with its strategy. Strategic planning specifies *what* will be accomplished by *when*. Organization structure specifies *who* will accomplish what and *how* it will be accomplished. Unfortunately, many banks stop after planning and try to implement new strategy as in "What's in it for me?" and "How to make a strategic decision" with an obsolete organization structure.

For many years we have heard bankers say, "Banks must become more market driven." "They must become more sales oriented." "They must become more customer oriented." Many of these calls for action and change have become so shopworn that they have now reached the state of cliches.

Of course banks must do things differently in the 1990s than in the past 50 years. No banker who faces the daily competition for funds and lending opportunities argues with those who urge an emphasis on the marketplace. And most bankers we know would readily assure anyone who asks them that they are indeed "market driven." But some bankers might be confusing what they intend to do with what they are actually doing. The evidence of a market-driven bank is more than rhetoric, it is more than good intentions. The evidence of its existence is a coherent bank strategy and a complementary organization structure that drives the bank in an unmistakable direction.

A market-driven bank does not just happen. A bank *becomes* market driven. And the process of becoming implies a change from one state of being to another state of being. For most banks the prior state includes not only a strategy that is no longer effective in a deregulated environment but also the organization structure that implements that strategy.

The purpose of organization structure is to reinforce and reward the behaviors that the strategy calls for. In each of the opening incidents, an outdated structure was reinforcing and rewarding behavior that was contrary to the strategy. It is important to understand that in each of the incidents, there were no bad guys. Each individual or department was behaving in their own best interests according to the organization structure that management had established. It was the organization structure, not people, that was getting in the way of the new strategies. The redirection of strategy in many banks is taking place within structures that simply do not fit the strategy. For most banks, substantial changes in bank strategy dictate that there must be substantial changes in the way banks design their organizations.

---

The biggest influence on how we behave at work and what we think is important, is how the work is structured.

---

While a well thought-out strategy is important, it does not guarantee that a bank will perform effectively. Implementation is at least as important. One of the most essential factors contributing to successful implementation is the overall design of the organization.

## WHAT IS ORGANIZATION STRUCTURE?

Think of organization structure as the anatomy of the bank. It provides a foundation within which the bank functions. The structure of a bank, similar to the anatomy of a human being, can be viewed as a framework. It is the framework of jobs and departments that directs the behavior of individuals and groups toward achieving management's objectives and strategies.

Organization structures enable bank managers to perform two important tasks. These tasks—specialization and coordination—comprise the process of designing an organization.[2] *Specialization* involves dividing the work of the bank into units in order to achieve efficient performances. *Coordination* involves integrating the objectives of specialized units in order to achieve the bank's strategic objectives. In very simple terms then, designing your bank's organization structure involves taking apart the work of the bank and putting it back together in a way that achieves the bank's strategic objectives. In practice, this procedure becomes much more complex, especially in the banking industry.

## TRADITIONAL BANK ORGANIZATION

To understand why organization structure is so critical to effective implementation we must examine how banks have traditionally been organized. With this understanding it will then be easier to see why problems exist with many present structures and what must be done to integrate bank strategy with bank organization structure.

Similar types of business organizations such as consumer product manufacturers and large retailers often have very similar organization structures. This unfortunately is not the case in banking. The reason is that banks vary in size as well as structure. In other words, banks perform similar functions, but may be large or small, be a unit bank or have 20 branches, be part of some holding company arrangement, or have only a few or several thousand employees. Yet, even with these constraints, bank organization structure has some basic concepts.[3] You must be familiar with these basic concepts if you are to improve the organization structure of your bank.

Generally, most banks are highly departmentalized, because the increase in volume, complexity, and number of services offered require specialized areas of knowledge. One individual cannot perform all the necessary tasks associated with a group of related activities. The managerial problems associated with departmentalization are directly related to the number of specialized jobs. Obviously the degree of departmentalization varies with the size and major activity of the bank. While all banks perform the same basic functions, only those with sufficient volume in a particular function will departmentalize.

There are two major categories for grouping jobs in any type of business: (1) based on internal operations or functions, and (2) based on output.

### Internal-Oriented Structures

Internal-oriented structures are based on the functions of the business. The basic functions of a manufacturing firm are production, finance, marketing, and accounting. A hospital consists of such functions as surgery, psychiatry, housekeeping,

**FIGURE 6-1**
**A Functional Organization Structure**

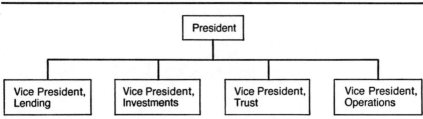

and pharmacy. The basic functions of a bank are loans, investments, operations, and trust. Thus, a *functional organization* is based on the activities or operations performed. A bank organized along functional lines is shown in Figure 6-1.

The identifying characteristic of function-oriented structures is the use of the functions of the business as the basis for identifying which departments will report to the CEO. The placement of these units at the highest level in the organization reflects the dominant concern of top management—to achieve operational efficiencies through the integration of the important functions of the business.

## Output-Oriented Structures

There are other ways to organize a business other than around internal functions. Traditionally, banks have not used such methods to organize at the very highest level of the organization. However, as we move down into the traditional bank structure we find other forms of organization. The three commonly used output-oriented forms, *product, geography*, and *market*, are oriented toward external factors.

### Product Departmentalization
This structure groups together all activities associated with a particular product or line of products. As a bank grows in size, it is difficult for one individual to coordinate the activities or be knowledgeable about a range of bank products. Grouping activities along product lines uses the specialized skills of people af-

**FIGURE 6–2**
**Organizing along Product Lines**

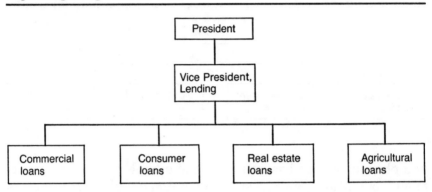

filiated with a particular product. Figure 6–2 illustrates this form of organization.

### *Geographic Departmentalization*
Obviously this structure groups activities according to location. It is often used in banks with physically dispersed markets or in those banks with branch systems, especially statewide banking. Figure 6–3 presents a geographical departmentalization.

### *Market Departmentalization*
This structure groups activities necessary to serve a particular group of customers. Let's suppose our hypothetical bank de-

**FIGURE 6–3**
**Organizing along Geographic Lines**

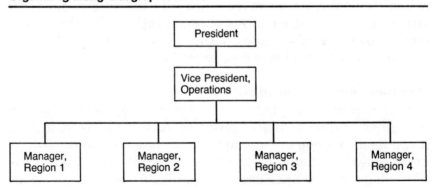

**FIGURE 6–4**
**Organizing along Market Lines**

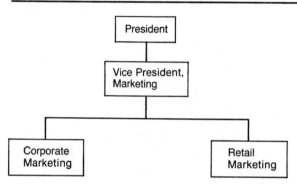

cided sometime during the 1970s that a marketing function was necessary. The new vice president decides to organize the department as shown in Figure 6–4, based on customers.

Figure 6–5 combines all the previous figures and gives us a general idea how a traditional bank's organization structure might have evolved. The bank may have continued to grow, becoming more complex as it added additional line and staff departments. But at the very highest level it remained organized around internal operations—the traditional banking functions of loans, investments, operations, and trust.

In fact, the use of the function-oriented design is so widespread in banking that veteran bankers usually refer to it as the "traditional" organizational form. Its popularity reflects its successful achievement of efficient operations.

Do not be concerned if your bank does not look exactly like the bank in Figure 6–5. That is not important. What is important is the realization that the traditional bank's organization structure was internal operations-oriented and that other ways of organizing based on external factors exist.

## THREE TRUTHS ABOUT ORGANIZATION STRUCTURE

Any bank manager whose goal is to develop a high-performance culture cannot achieve that goal with an ineffective or-

**FIGURE 6–5**
**Mixed Departmentalization**

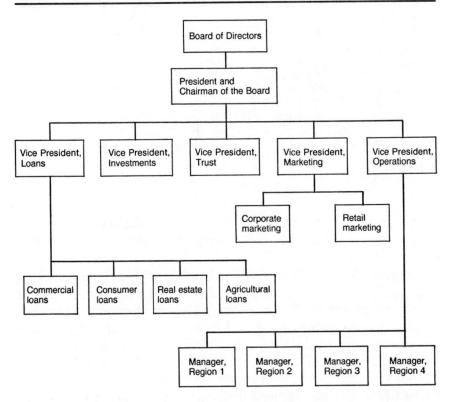

ganization structure. In this regard there are three universal truths:

**1.** *An effective organization structure does not result from chance or historical accident.* A crucial management responsibility is to deliberately devise an organization structure that supports and is complementary with the bank's strategy, technology, and competitive environment.

The redirection of strategy in many banks is taking place within organization structures that simply do not fit the strategy.

**2.** *With the passage of time, organization structures seem to take on lives of their own; they become ingrained and resistant to change.*     Each of the three chapter-opening incidents clearly illustrate this truth. The tendency of organization structures to perpetuate themselves undoubtedly has led author Tom Peters to make the rather bold recommendation that "if you aren't reorganizing, pretty substantially, once every 6 to 12 months, you're probably out of step with the times."[4]

**3.** *There is no one best organization structure for a bank.* The appropriate structure will vary. The challenge to management is to design the appropriate structure that facilitates getting work done, and done well. The organization structures in "That's not my job" and "What's in it for me?" impeded getting work done. The secretary in the Women's Bank and the young calling officer were unable to do their best work because the structure of their banks got in the way.

## WHEN IS ORGANIZATION STRUCTURE A PROBLEM?

If the ultimate purpose of an organization structure is to facilitate getting work done, then, whenever the work is not done well, or at all, one of the potential causes can be the organization structure. If any of the following situations occur on a regular basis, look to your bank's organization structure as the cause.[5]

### Conflict between Groups

Conflict between departments or groups within the bank is an important indicator of structure problems. The conflict might be the result of personality clashes between key people, but it can also be the result of differences in basic goals and means for achieving them. The organization structure is particularly suspect if the conflict arises out of disagreement between the goals of the departments, rather than disagreement over the goals of the bank.

• We are familiar with a large bank where when the level of deposits for an individual customer reaches a certain level the customer is moved to the trust department. However, the deposit goals of the branch manager are not reduced accordingly. The branch manager must find a way to make up the difference. Thus, there is no incentive for a branch manager to encourage customers to place deposits above the ceiling amount. In fact, there have been several instances where customers were encouraged by branch managers to place deposits in competitor institutions so that the branch would not lose a customer. Management is unaware of these practices.

• The head of retail banking in a medium-size bank was given the task of increasing deposits in a fairly short period of time. One of the ways he planned to do it was through a certificate of deposit promotion to upscale retail customers. In the process, he needed the names of the bank's best customers which he requested from the head of the trust department. Two weeks later he had not received the list. When asked again, the trust department head refused to provide the list to the retail banker.

Finally, in "What's in it for me?" the outcome was that the young calling officer did not get the discount on the loan and the customer left his deposits where they were and secured a loan from another bank.

The important thing to note in each of these situations is that the problems are the result of conflicts between the goals of individual departments, not the goals of the bank. More important, however, is that the biggest loser in each conflict was *the bank.* If the conflicts between departments in your bank result in the bank being the big loser, you can say with certainty that the problem lies in the bank's organization structure.

In "What's in it for me?" the customer did not lose anything, the calling officer lost nothing (except perhaps some motivation), and the commercial lender lost nothing. The only loser was the bank. Somewhere in his MBA program, the calling officer probably learned that the purpose of an organization structure was to facilitate getting work done. He has now found out that in this bank, it **will** impede him from doing his job.

Finally, such a bank will most likely not implement its new sales strategy to its fullest potential with its existing organization structure, no matter how hard it tries or how many times it alters the strategy. So the bank loses all around.

## Problems in Coordinating Work between Groups

An important indicator of organization design problems is difficulty in coordinating work between departments.

• The mortgage lending group of a medium-size bank developed a detailed sales plan which utilized the bank branches as referral centers. Each branch was expected to produce a certain number of prospects based on its location. One branch was expected to be particularly productive because of its location. Three months into the program, the branch had not produced one referral. The head of mortgage lending phoned the branch manager to inquire if there were any problems. The branch manager's reply was, "It's not in my goals—if you want it done then get it into my goals."

• In a large West Coast bank, a very good customer asked his lending officer if he could wire his mother in Taiwan. The customer had $800,000 on deposit in the bank and a $1 million line of credit. The lending officer inquired of a person in the bank's international department and was told that the international department would not do it until they saw evidence that the customer would be service charged.

Finally each of our three chapter-opening incidents illustrates a definite lack of coordination between groups. The loan application was not completed, the calling officer could not bring in new business, and a bank made a strategic decision to add two credit cards, simply because departments were unable to coordinate their efforts. In each case, the organization structure was the behind-the-scenes cause of the problem.

## Slowness in Adapting to Change

The neglect or avoidance of change and of needed innovation can be an indicator of organization structure problems.

• One bank carefully planned an offensive strategy for its middle market. It had developed what was believed to be an innovative cash management product for middle-market businesses and expected great results from its efforts. Things began to break down when it came time to implement the strategy. The commercial lending department believed that it was the natural home for the product since the commercial lender had primary contact with the customers. The trust department disagreed. They reasoned that since they would be managing the funds, the product should be housed in the trust department. The operations department disagreed. They reasoned that since they would be handling all of the transactions, the product should be housed with them. All of this took place almost three years ago. To date the product has not been introduced.

The above happens far too often in most banks. Many banks have developed innovative new products and strategies that for some reason never reach implementation. The demise of an innovative new product or strategy often begins with the question, "Where are we going to put it?" The resulting conflict over which group will manage the program takes precedence over the program itself. Consequently, effective implementation never occurs or occurs poorly; an opportunity is missed, a competitive advantage lost.

In "How to make a strategic decision," it took several months of infighting before the CEO decided on an implementation strategy which gave both departments their own credit card. This incredible incident resulted in poor implementation and as a bank officer told us:

> The result was that it appeared that we were playing a new game: stump the customer.

All of the incidents reported in this chapter resulted in slow, poor, or no response to change and necessary innovation. Each was caused by problems in organization structure.

---

The evidence of a market-driven bank is a coherent bank strategy and a complementary organization structure that drives the bank in an unmistakable direction.

---

## Ambiguous Job Assignments

When employees of a bank are constantly asking what goals to pursue, where to find needed information, or what work to concentrate on, the organization structure may be at fault. The branch manager referred to above was in effect asking the head of mortgage lending what goals he was expected to pursue. Managers are often tempted to blame people in these circumstances or to question their commitment to the bank. It was not the branch manager's fault that he did not know what goals to pursue. On the other hand, the mortgage banker was put in an equally frustrating position.

• One large bank actually had two cash management products housed in two different departments. Members of each department were forbidden to tell the customer about the existence of the other cash management product unless the customer was going to leave the bank. We have seen so many instances of this situation that we have labeled such products "mystery products." These are products that are apparently a secret. No one is supposed to know about them except employees. It is doubtful that any other industry has mystery products. Most businesses want their customers to know about all of the products the firm makes available to them. Their existence in the banking industry is just another indication of organization structure problems in many banks.

## THE RESULTS OF ORGANIZATION STRUCTURE PROBLEMS

Each of the banks discussed so far in this chapter is feeling the effects, knowingly or unknowingly, of problems in their organization structure. This is not to say that management has diagnosed the problem as such. They may have diagnosed it as problems with people, personality clashes, uncommitted employees, or turf battles that are a natural part of a bank. This is not the case. The end results of organization structure problems are tangible and observable in most banks.

   **1.** *The bank is a collection of semiautonomous operating units.* Most new strategies such as relationship banking, financial planning, cash management, personal banking, and the development of a sales culture, require a pulling together throughout the bank. Unfortunately, there is usually little linkage between such functions as trust, commercial lending, retail banking, and funds management. There may be cross-selling within functions but a true sales culture demands it be done across functions. As one senior banker told us:

> We must find a way to bring all of the resources of our bank to bear on the problems of customers.

The banker who made this statement was expressing his frustration in the inability of his bank to do what it needed to do, and had the capabilities to do  He continued·

> We have the skills and capabilities to do everything we must do to be a full-service financial services firm. Unfortunately, we have been unable to do it. I don't know why. We keep trying and trying again but it seems that we are our own worst enemy  We can't seem to make it click

Trying to re-implement a revised strategy with an inappropriate organization structure will, as we know from a previous chapter, only result in continued trouble or even failure. This banker's frustration will unfortunately continue for as long as his bank's organization structure is incapable of implementing its strategy of transforming itself into a full-service financial services firm. And right now, he is unaware of the reason why.

Each of the three banks in our chapter opening incidents illustrate this outcome. The problems of the secretary, new calling officer, and the two-card bank happened because the three banks were little more than a collection of semiautonomous operating units—pursuing their own and often conflicting strategies.

**2.** *The bank's organization structure dictates its strategy.* One of the most important principles of management is that strategy should dictate structure. Simply, you decide what you want to do and then organize to do it. If a bank allows its structure to dictate its strategy then it is, in effect, allowing how it is organized to determine what it does. And that violates an important principle of management.

In case after case in this chapter, we have seen what happens when organization structure dictates a bank's actions. One bank never launched a promising innovative cash management product, a mortgage lender was unable to fully implement a bank strategy, one bank's employees were unable to tell their customers about the existence of another of the bank's products. Finally, in "How to make a strategic decision," the bank's structure dictated that it have two credit cards.

**3.** *Only strategies compatible with the existing organization structure are accepted.* An unfortunate result of allowing structure to dictate strategy is that it severely limits the strategies a bank can pursue successfully. In actuality, the bank is unable to do anything unless it is compatible with the existing organization structure. It is easy to see that in such cases, innovation and change are very difficult.

Most proposed new bank products as well as strategies cut across the traditional banking functions. In the past, the various banking functions offered their own products which made it possible for banks to be organized for their convenience and not the convenience of the customer. It was the customer who was expected to be inconvenienced, being forced to deal with several bank functions to satisfy his or her total needs. Today, however, the typical customer's needs cut across the banking functions and products and approaches designed to satisfy these needs must do the same.

Unfortunately, the traditional bank organization structure is not compatible with successfully implementing many of today's products and strategies, and if only those strategies that are compatible are accepted, effectiveness will be severely limited. The effectiveness of the bank in "How to make a strategic decision" will be limited if it must force every new strategy that it pursues to conform with its organization structure. The result thus far has been that the bank's structure has forced it to have two credit cards without any consideration given to whether it should have two cards, or the impact on its customers of having to deal with two different departments. Clearly, bank managers must integrate bank strategy with bank organization structure.

# CHAPTER 7

## MAKING YOUR OWN WAY: INTEGRATING BANK STRATEGY AND STRUCTURE

*The only stability is stability in motion.*
John W. Gardner

One factor that keeps many banks from realizing their full potential and from unleashing the full capabilities of their technological and human resources is the organizational structure of the bank. What often gets blamed on people—personality clashes, turf battles, uncommitted employees, and departments competing with each other to the detriment of the bank— really has nothing to do with "bad people." It has to do with "bad management." An effective organization structure enables qualified people to do their best work. And it is management's responsibility to devise it.

A great deal has been written about the importance of strategy and strategy development in banking. Bankers have been berated for having unclear strategies in response to the changing industry environment. While well thought-out strategy is important, it does not guarantee that a bank will perform effectively. To implement, management must coordinate the individual specialized efforts of people and do it well. Thus, we need both a clear strategy and a compatible organization design. The message of the last chapter should be clear: One of the most essential factors contributing to successful implementation is how the bank is structured. Integrating bank strategy and structure is the subject of this chapter.[1]

## IMPORTANT FEATURES OF
## ORGANIZATION STRUCTURES

Most people who work in organizations tend to think of structure in rather narrow terms. We think in terms of our own job responsibilities and duties, whom we report to, whom we must please, and whether we have enough authority to do our job. In other words we think of structure in terms of our job. While this is certainly meaningful, it is too narrow a view for a manager. A manager must think in terms that describe the entire structure itself, not the jobs that comprise it. Three ideas are critical here: (1) how *specialized* is the organization, (2) how *centralized* is the organization, and (3) how *formalized* is the organization.

1. *Specialization* is the degree to which the overall task has been divided among the different jobs. The more extensive the division of work, the more highly specialized is the structure.
2. *Centralization* is the degree to which the authority to make decisions is concentrated in the jobs of those in top management. As authority is delegated downward, the structure becomes less centralized, and more decentralized.
3. *Formalization* is the degree to which rules, policies, and procedures exist. The more extensive the rules and procedures, the more formalized the structure.

A bank can be described as being more or less specialized, centralized, and formalized than another bank. We hear all the time that a particular bank is highly centralized and formal while another is more decentralized and informal. But to say that bank organization structures are different really doesn't mean anything unless the differences make a difference. There must be a relationship between a bank's organization structure and its performance.

## EVOLVING BANK ORGANIZATION STRUCTURES

A great many varieties of organization structures exist in banking. A bank may be organized in ways that reflect its personnel strength, history, tradition, and legal requirements. One of the largest banks in the country has been organized around the personal interests of the three men who run it. However, the many varieties will almost always tend toward two general types: the *function-oriented* structure and more recently, the *market-oriented* structure.

There is no doubt that when a bank opened its doors for the first time four or five decades ago, the first two business functions that needed to be developed were: (1) *operations*—to receive and account for deposits, and (2) *loans*. They may have been handled by one or two persons but eventually, as the bank grew, these two functions became the primary departments reporting to the CEO. Thus, as a result of historical practice and industry educational programs, operations and lending specialists reached high levels of expertise and efficiency.

As the bank grew, the strategy of efficiency of operations continued. In response to the increased workload of more customers and services, management created additional specialized functional units. Trust and investment functions were usually the first new departments to be added once the bank passed the $50 million asset mark. As more time passed and skilled personnel were hired, an asset management function might have emerged. With more growth, the function-oriented structure became exceedingly complex until, depending on the size of the bank, departments representing the functions of lending, operations, investments, and trust, reported to the CEO of the typical bank.

### The Function-Oriented Structure

Why was the functional structure so widespread in banking for 40 years? Very simply, because it was the correct one. The functional organization structure is the most effective design under two conditions:

1. The environment the business faces is stable, certain, and predictable.
2. The major strategic objective is efficient processing of internal information and tight controls over internal processes.

For decades then, the organization structure of most banks was compatible with and supportive of its major strategic objectives related to efficiency of operations.

---

Maximum bank performance is attained when there is harmony between strategy and structure.

---

The function-oriented structure achieves its best results in a situation where stable performance of a routine task is important. Because they are highly *specialized, centralized,* and *formalized,* they encourage and reward employees for "doing things right," for being efficient. In such a structure, management can define the expected activities and decisions of employees with great precision and detail. The discretion in each employee's contribution to overall objectives is purposely limited and employees are encouraged to achieve accuracy and efficiency in every department and job. The routineness of day-to-day activities enables managers to develop extensive rules and procedures to govern nearly every action and decision. Finally, the specialization at both the organizational and individual level develops employees with narrow expertise which facilitates training.

Thus, as long as the industry remained regulated, banking was a relatively simple business. Management could focus its attention inward and the function-oriented structure worked well.

### Things Begin to Change

The 1970s was a time of turbulence in banking. In retrospect, it might be called an age of discontinuity, since it marked the passage of many long-standing traditions and operational patterns. Some of the developments have had a major impact on the strategy and structure of banks today.[2] For example:

- With improvements in technology, the efficient processing of internal information is no longer the problem it once was, and control of bank funds can be accomplished more efficiently in less time.
- The emergence of electronic banking and the stepping up of the technology revolution in banking has made traditional time and space barriers obsolete.
- Inflationary pressures that took borrowers, savers, and investors on an interest-rate roller coaster led to the phasing out of Regulation Q and administered pricing and the phasing in of market-driven pricing.
- The delay in coordinating the price banks could legally pay for consumer deposits and market prices precipitated disintermediation of consumer funds, *and*, not so incidentally, caused customer relationships to move away from depository institutions and into the hand of non-bank competitors.
- Disintermediation not only brought Merrill Lynch and others into the banking business, it upset the stability of the thrift-housing infrastructure, dependent as it was on borrowing short and lending long. One consequence was that thrift institutions battled hard and with much success to obtain such traditional banking powers as checking accounts and consumer lending.
- Inflationary pressure and its spawning of disintermediation, combined with the resulting changes in pricing structures, also impacted bank balance sheets. As spreads narrowed, more and more banks and holding companies turned their attention to fee-income opportunities. This shift in turn caused a fresh appraisal of banking's product line.
- Competition within the banking industry not only intensified, but increasingly and more directly banks found themselves competing in *the financial services business*. They could no longer count on such traditional product-line exclusives as the checking account or the credit

card, or even their singular dominance of the corporate lending field.

In sum, the turbulence of the past has forced a change in traditional thinking about strategy and operational patterns in most banks.

## *Advantages Become Disadvantages*

As the environment changed, the necessity for new bank strategies developed. Unfortunately, the advantages of the functional structure rapidly become disadvantages when the environment becomes unstable and unpredictable, requiring a flexible and responsive organization structure.

By virtue of their emphasis on efficient operations, function-oriented structures reward continuation of the tried-and-true ways of doing things. Over time the chain of command evolves into a lengthy one, with many different managerial positions and levels that supervise people doing rather narrowly specialized jobs. Individual discretion, initiative, and creativity have been discouraged because detailed job descriptions and specifications have removed the necessity for independent judgment. Employees have learned that they are paid to do their jobs according to the rules and restrict their attention to those matters for which they are directly accountable, also known as the "That's not my job" attitude. (Such attitudes are most obvious in those types of organizations which have implemented the purest form of the functional structure—a bureaucracy.)

By their very nature, functional structures attract people who value certainty and closure. Adventuresome and entrepreneurial people either leave the organization or lose their zeal. Ordinarily, the structure does not encourage the development of people who can cope with the demands of a competitive environment. This self-selection process is the basic cause of the inability of the function-oriented structure to deal with change.

The longer it is in existence, the more likely it is to take on a life of its own. When this occurs, identification with the culture of the function (e.g., "I'm a trust person," "I'm in operations") may be more important than with the culture of the bank, if one exists, which is unlikely. In the last chapter we saw many instances where bank goals were sacrificed to department goals. In such situations, the CEO eventually becomes a referee of turf squabbles among competing functional specialties.

Finally, the functional structure artificially segments customers and frustrates them. As long as the structure is in place, the bank remains organized for the convenience of the bank, not the customer.

---

If the business-as-usual strategy will not work, then the traditional functional structure will not work.

---

### Banking Adds Another Function

Trying to be flexible and maneuverable with a quasi-bureaucratic, inflexible organization is no easy task. Most banks coped with the first signs of competitive challenge by turning to the marketing function. Although many banks adopted marketing terminology in the 1960s, it was not until the late 1970s that the functioning of these departments changed substantially. In most instances the marketing function already existed, but its primary purposes were advertising and public relations. During the 1980s, many large banks organized their marketing departments along market lines—retail, trust, corporate, and even international division marketing managers. Some organized the department along product lines—deposit services, lending services, asset-based financing, and cash management services.

Also during the late 1970s and 1980s, most banks elevated the new function to an organizational level on par with loans, investments, operations, and trust. In most banks, however, this occurred only on the organization chart. In many banks the operational efficiency orientation remains deeply embedded, and when key strategic decisions are made, they reflect internal operations rather than external market and competitive effectiveness criteria.

The appearance during the last 15 years of marketing departments in the structure of operations-dominated and function-oriented banks reflects a transitional state. This transitional state can last as long as competitive pressures permit and as long as management takes to recognize the deficiencies of the functional structure. If the competitive pressures are intense and result in deterioration of the customer base, the functional structure becomes increasingly incompatible with strategies necessary to make the bank competitive.

Maximum bank performance is attained when there is harmony between strategy and structure. For most banks, therefore, the functional structure is now incompatible with the environment it must compete in. A prime leadership responsibility is to take an active role in transforming the bank's structure from the traditional functional structure to a market-oriented structure. This transformation will require commitment, talent, and time.

---

An effective organization structure enables qualified people to do their best work.

---

## The Market-Oriented Structure

The dominant characteristic of a market-oriented structure is the elevation of customer- and market-based departments to top organizational levels. This means that departments representing groups of customers, not the traditional banking functions, report to the CEO. Units whose primary concern is satisfying product and customer concerns are placed at the top of the organization. All products and functions necessary to serve a particular group of customers are housed in one department.

In banks that are beginning to adopt this structure, market-oriented departments such as commercial banking, retail banking, and real estate banking report directly to the CEO. An example is provided in Figure 7–1. This particular bank refers to corporate, retail, and real estate banking as its three "external businesses." Funds management and operations are referred to as "internal businesses." Obviously, other banks

**FIGURE 7-1**
**A Market-Oriented Structure**

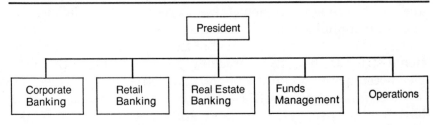

have different market units, such as energy, argricultural, and equine, depending on their particular markets.

Placing market-oriented units at the top of the organization reflects implicitly or explicitly the strategy of top management—*to be in the right markets with the right products at the right time.*

For an organization trying to adapt to a continually changing environment, the market-oriented structure offers several advantages:

- The organization now looks outward to its markets rather than inward to its functions.
- The chain of command is relatively short, with fewer management positions than exist in the function-oriented structure.
- Middle management tends to disappear as employees begin to understand and accept the overall goals of the bank rather than function-oriented goals.

In contrast to function-oriented structures, they are relatively *less specialized, less centralized,* and *less formalized.* The typical job is broader in scope, with greater latitude for individual discretion. Jobs are defined in terms of expected outcomes (results) rather than required activities (efforts). Because employees understand their contribution to the overall objectives of the bank, disputes are settled according to bank, not departmental, objectives. Decision making is done by those people who have the expertise to solve the problem at hand. The primary criterion for participating in decision making is expertise, not position in the hierarchy. Shared understandings of what is expected replace rules and procedures. These are the organizational characteristics that are absolutely necessary to deal with change.

Some new jobs appear in the market-oriented structure, such as market managers, product managers, and sales personnel. These jobs can be found in function-oriented structures, but they really only attain their fullest potential in organizations that have made a clear commitment to market development.

Market-oriented structures are designed to work well in uncertain, unpredictable, and unstable environments. If they are functioning at their best, they encourage every employee to be problem solving, sales oriented, and committed to corporate-wide purposes. In this structure there is no personal advantage to protecting one's specialized turf. The departmentalized mentality fostered by functional specialization is hopefully supplanted by organizational commitment.

Of course, market-oriented structures do have some disadvantages:

- There is some loss of efficiency. They do not take maximum advantage of the economies of specialization, since the dominant jobs in the structure are relatively less specialized. Employees must obviously be competent in their specialties, but they must also have knowledge of all products, services, and operational aspects. Strategies such as relationship banking and cross-selling require breadth of knowledge, as well as an understanding of the needs of the customer.
- The use of group decision making and delegated authority usually involves greater time and effort than one-person centralized decision making.
- The less use of rules and procedures often involves trial-and-error testing of solutions to problems, and new strategies.

These costs are inherent in the market-oriented structure, but the loss of efficiency is more than offset by the increase in effectiveness.

Finally, in an ideal market-oriented structure, the managers of the market groups would have profit responsibility for serving that market. This assumes that profit accountability focuses on markets, not products. For a bank this would mean that accounting would have to assign the profitability of every customer to a market unit. Of the many banks who have adopted the market-oriented structure, few have yet to develop this capability. However, many of these market-oriented structures are in the early stages of evolution and will ultimately evolve to the point where they are able to take full advantage of all of the benefits of the structure.

Figure 7–2 compares the function-oriented structure and the market-oriented structure. You should view these two types as extremes on a continuum that contains many shades of differences. Remember that there is no one organization structure appropriate for all banks. The appropriate structure for your bank depends upon its primary strategy. If adaptiveness and flexibility are the key to performance in your bank, then you must consider the market-oriented structure. Most banks really don't have a choice. The business-as-usual strategy will simply not work. And if that strategy will not work, traditional function-oriented structures will not work.

### How One Bank Reorganized around Markets

This section illustrates how one bank's retail unit reorganized itself toward a market-oriented structure. The changes in this bank's retail business were the most dramatic, and they provide us with a great opportunity to illustrate vividly what happens when a bank decides to organize around groups of customers rather than banking functions.

Figure 7–3 presents the basic structure of the bank prior to reorganization, with the retail-related products and functions shown in dotted boxes. This bank was organized like most banks (large and small) in the United States, and therefore could represent nearly any institution. Departments representing banking functions reported to the president and it was quite possible that a retail customer's business could be spread across all four organizational units. In this particular situation, it was unlikely that one function was fully aware of a custom-

**FIGURE 7–2**
**Evolving Bank Organization Structures**

| From | | To |
|---|---|---|
| Function oriented | | Market oriented |
| | *Appropriate Strategy* | |
| Efficiency of operations | | Effectiveness and competitive strength |
| | *Compatible Environment* | |
| Stable, predictable, certain | | Unstable, unpredictable, uncertain |
| | *Dominant Characteristics* | |
| Highly specialized | | Less specialized |
| Highly centralized | | More decentralized |
| Highly formalized | | Less formalized |
| | *Secondary Characteristics* | |
| Activities-oriented job descriptions | | Results-oriented job descriptions |
| Lengthy chain of command | | Shorter chain of command |
| Functional departments report to CEO | | Product/market units report to CEO |

er's total relationships with the institution, and no one unit was responsible for the bank's retail customers.

Figure 7–3 clearly illustrates the disadvantages of the function-oriented structure in today's banking environment. The bank found it extremely difficult to implement any new strategic directions in retail banking, including a sales culture and personal banking as well as any type of innovative reward system such as incentive compensation.

Finally, all of the problems discussed in the last chapter—conflicting goals, difficulty in coordinating work, ambiguous job assignments, and slowness in adapting to change—were all present to one degree or another. As far as the retail customer

**FIGURE 7–3**

**Basic Structure prior to Reorganization (dotted lines indicate retail-related products and functions)**

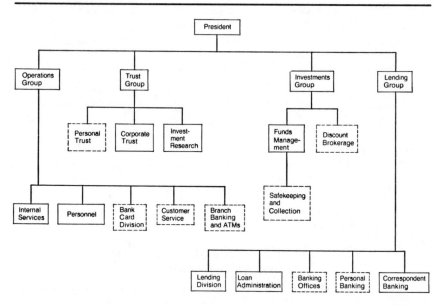

was concerned, the bank was indeed a collection of semiautonomous operating units organized for its own convenience.

Figure 7–4 presents the retail bank as it is presently structured. It shows how the retail work of the bank has been taken apart, and put back together in such a way to implement its new strategy of becoming a truly market-driven financial institution.

Management believes that the new structure will now enable people to do their best work as the bank strives to become market driven, in contrast to the previous structure which often hindered work being done in this direction. In the retail bank, groups of customers are represented in two departments: executive and private banking which also includes the retail portion of the former trust function, and personal banking.

This structure has all the advantages of market-oriented structures. The retail bank is now clearly organized for the convenience of the customer and not the bank. Intergroup conflicts

**FIGURE 7–4**
**Present Structure of the Retail Bank**

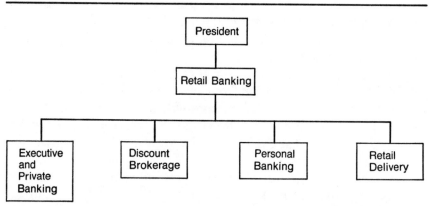

caused by differences in goals between functions have been significantly reduced. The new structure encourages coordination of all the retail functions because they are no longer part of what were often competing departments. Turf fights have lessened greatly, and cross-selling, product development, and innovative reward systems have been far more effective. Finally, the retail bank as a unit of the entire organization has been able to respond more quickly to changes in the market and to competitive moves.

A prime leadership responsibility is to take an active role in transforming the traditional functional structure to a market-oriented structure.

## MANAGERS MUST MANAGE ORGANIZATION STRUCTURE

Organization structure dramatically influences bank performance. Management must, therefore, carefully manage structure. In the last chapter we saw many instances where structure was permitted to manage management. The existing structure is always a strong force for stability. People become comfortable in their jobs. They quite naturally resist threatened disruption to the status quo. Thus, the benefit of stability can become a detriment when change is necessary in the bank's organization structure.

We know from the two chapters on managing change that while the details will differ from instance to instance, the general principles of successful change will be the same regardless of the specific setting. The following five principles will greatly improve the odds that a change in your bank's organization structure will succeed.

1. *There is no quick-fix solution to structure problems.* Top management must fully appreciate the impact of organization structure on bank performance and be committed to changing it. Evidence of this commitment is willingness to become actively involved in all of the processes required to bring it about. If training and retraining are required, top management is in the classroom along with everyone else. If goal setting is part of the required change, top management sets their goals. Changing a structure involves changing all jobs in some way, including top management. When a change in structure is required, there is no quick fix.

One key indicator that a change in structure is required is when managers acknowledge that they do not have the people necessary to implement a particular strategy. "We can't compete with the brokers and insurance companies because we don't have the horses" is an example. The reason that they do not have the people is that function-oriented structures do not provide for such skills and talents. A quick-fix solution would be to go out and hire salespeople and financial planners and graft their functions onto the present structure. This will not work because the bank culture has created an ingrained preference for operations.

A commitment to change structure usually occurs after management has rejected the quick fix. These managers understand that structure is a principal source of employees' beliefs of what is right, what is expected, and what is rewarded. The banking industry is overflowing with accounts of failed efforts to bring about change. The most often cited reason for failure is that top managers were either not committed to the effort or that they did not demonstrate their commitment by word and, most importantly, by deed.

**2.** *Establish your strategy, then test the adequacy of your structure to implement it.* Strategy must precede structure. What may seem obvious in the abstract often becomes less obvious in reality. For example, every strategic planning effort begins with an analysis of the environment, followed by the distinctive strengths of the bank. But existing bank organization structures have seen to it that the distinctive strengths of most banks are operations related. There is a tendency to permit the operations-oriented competency to overwhelm signal after signal that a change in strategy is necessary. To avoid this urge, establish the appropriateness of your strategy, then test the adequacy of your structure to implement it.

**3.** *Persistence pays off.* The third principle requires persistence in explaining and promoting the necessity for a change in structure. It took the bank in this chapter over three years to bring about the change in its structure. Citicorp's reorganization involved a change for nearly all of its 52,000 employees. Former chairman Walter Wriston described it as "the greatest financial revolution in American history."[3]

Highly visible managers who relentlessly articulate the importance of the bank's strategy for the future are indispensable elements of success.

**4.** *A more imaginative and effective reward system.* The fourth principle is to reward the behavior called for by the new strategy and structure. Rewards must be directed to the people whose performance is consistent with the new strategy. This principle, similar to the first three, is deceptively simple. But common knowledge and common sense tell us that pay, promotion, status, and privilege are historically founded and tradition bound. Your bank's present reward system reflects all that management has previously considered to be valuable. In addition, the system has built-in safeguards to protect employees from changes in criteria. Yet criteria must change and the system must change. Implementing this principle requires managerial courage, as well as persistence.

Compensation and promotion present particular difficulties in market-oriented structures. There are fewer levels in the hierarchy and, consequently, fewer opportunities for upward promotion. Compensation plans must be more carefully devised to reflect real contributions to strategic objectives among employees at the same level. More than likely they will involve incentive and bonus compensation plans and rethinking the awarding of traditional management perks. We have seen that when management's attitude toward compensation reflects accomplishment rather than authority, it is possible to develop more imaginative and effective reward systems.

**5.** *Allow sufficient time.* The fifth principle, clearly illustrated in our example, is the importance of time. You do not change an organization structure overnight. If in the interest of time, a new organization structure is forced upon employees, they are unlikely to buy into it. And management's enthusiasm is unlikely to persuade them that the change is good for them. Our guidelines for managing change presented in Chapters 4 and 5 would be useful at this point.

How quickly a bank moves from operations-oriented strategies to market-oriented strategies depends on the market conditions it faces. The same can be said for organization structure. The only constant across all banks is that once management has defined and devised a strategy, its realization is made possible by the organization structure.

# PART 5

# REALIZING THE FUTURE

Part of human nature resents change, loves equilibrium, while another part welcomes novelty, loves the excitement of disequilibrium. There is no formula for the resolution of this tug-of-war, but it is obvious that absolute surrender to either of them invites disaster.

*J. Bartlet Brebner*

# CHAPTER 8

---

# THE CHALLENGE: DEVELOPING THE NEW BANKER

---

*Leadership is a part of management but not all of it. . . . Management activities such as planning, organizing, and decision making are dormant cocoons until the leader triggers the power of motivation in people and guides them toward goals.*

Keith Davis

At this point you might be asking the question "What was wrong with the old banker?" The answer, of course, is nothing. Indeed, we found many "old" bankers who are also effective managers and leaders. The age of the manager was not important. Neither, incidentally, was the size of the bank, the scope of the business, the age of the bank, nor the manager's years of experience in banking or primary area of banking expertise.

What was important was the manager's understanding that managing in today's bank is different from managing in yesterday's bank. Managing in the old bank required a particular set of skills. Managing in the new bank requires those same skills plus some new and equally important ones.

This concluding chapter provides a brief review of some of the most important characteristics of successful and unsuccessful managers and leaders. While this always makes for interesting reading, we will not stop here. It should be clear that we believe the development of competent bankers who are also effective managers and leaders is one of the critical human resource challenges facing the banking industry. The responsibility for developing the new banker rests in three places:

- The challenge to the banker.
- The challenge to the bank.
- The challenge to the industry

## THE ELUSIVE MANAGER-LEADER

Managers, whether they are CEOs, division managers, or branch managers, influence attitudes and expectations that encourage or discourage peak performance, gain or lose employee commitment, reward or penalize achievement. People relate to leaders. We see this every day as we make judgments about the leaders of sports teams, government agencies, and educational institutions. Leadership does make a difference.

Unfortunately, despite decades of studying leadership, psychologists are unable to state that there is one best way to lead. True leadership involves noncoercive types of influence to motivate others to accomplish some goal and effective communication is involved in the process. Leadership is not domination and intimidation. It results when a person influences others to accept his or her request without the exertion of power.

### Some Traits of Successful Leaders

There are some traits that are characteristic of successful leaders. A summary of some of the most studied traits is presented in Figure 8–1.[1] While leadership success is not entirely a function of these traits, to have such traits contributes to leadership success. While no one set of traits fits all leaders, Figure 8–1 gives us a good idea of the most important personal characteristics.

### Some Traits of Charismatic Leaders

Lately, a specific type of leader has received a great deal of attention: the charismatic or transformational leader. Franklin D. Roosevelt, John F. Kennedy, Martin Luther King, Jr., Mother Teresa, and Lee Iacocca are leaders who influenced through charisma.[2] Some people believe charismatic leaders

**FIGURE 8–1**
**Some Traits of Effective Leaders**

| Intelligence | Personality | Abilities |
|---|---|---|
| Judgment | Adaptability | Ability to enlist cooperation |
| Decisiveness | Alertness | Cooperativeness |
| Knowledge | Creativity | Popularity and prestige |
| Fluency of speech | Personal integrity | Interpersonal skills |
| | Self-confidence | Social participation |
| | Emotional control | Tact and diplomacy |
| | Independence | |

are needed to transform faltering or failing banks into vibrant, high-performance organizations. Transformational leaders succeed by:

1. Raising the level of consciousness of employees about the importance and value of certain goals, or vision.
2. Getting them to transcend self-interest for the sake of the team, or vision.
3. Generating trust among employees.
4. Convincing others to extend themselves and to develop new skills or improve existing ones.

Transformational leaders are said to have four important personal characteristics:[3]

- Dominance.
- Self-confidence.
- A need to influence.
- Conviction of moral righteousness.

An often cited example of transformational leadership is Lee Iacocca in the early 1980s at Chrysler Corporation. He helped transform a firm that was ready to go out of business into one that earned record profits. He accomplished this great feat by raising the level of consciousness of employees at all levels of the organization, having them focus on specific goals, building their trust in his vision, and encouraging them through effective communication to work harder.

Being told what we need to do and be is one thing. Becoming it
is another thing entirely

## Some Traits of Unsuccessful Leaders

The Center for Creative Leadership, a nonprofit research and
educational institution in Greensboro, North Carolina, was
formed to improve the practice of management. Two of the center's researchers, Morgan McCall, Jr., and Michael Lombardo,
have studied the differences between successful and unsuccessful managers.

They studied 21 *derailed managers*—successful people
who were expected to go higher in the organization, but who
reached a plateau late in their careers, were fired, or were
forced to retire early. They also studied 20 *arrivers*—those
who made it all the way to the top.[4] To their surprise, the two
groups had somewhat similar characteristics. Every one of the
41 managers possessed strengths, and every one had one or
more weaknesses. More often than any other flaw, insensitivity
to others was cited as a reason for derailment. But it was never
the only reason. Most often, a combination of personal qualities
and external circumstances put an end to the manager's rise.

The 10 most frequently found traits of unsuccessful managers were:
1. Insensitive to others; abrasive, intimidating, bullying
   style.
2. Cold, aloof, arrogant.
3. Betrayal of trust.
4. Overly ambitious; thinking of next job, playing poli-
   tics.
5. Specific performance problems with the business.
6. Overmanaging; unable to delegate or build a team.
7. Unable to staff effectively.
8. Unable to think strategically.
9. Unable to adapt to boss with different style.
10. Overdependent on mentor.

When the arrivers and the derailed were compared, a few identifiable differences showed up. Derailed managers often were described by peers as moody or volatile under pressure. Also, although neither group made many mistakes, all the arrivers handled theirs with poise and grace. Derailed managers tended to react to failure by going on the defensive, trying to keep it under wraps while they fixed it or, once the problem was visible, blaming it on someone else. Finally, the arrivers had the ability to get along with all types of people. They were direct but diplomatic. Arrivers also were outspoken but did not offend people in the process.

What can we conclude from the discussion of the traits of successful leaders, transformational leaders, and unsuccessful leaders? The very definite conclusion is that managers and leaders are like the rest of us: a patchwork of strengths and weaknesses. There is no one best, surefire, quick-fix way to success as a manager.

## Hope for the Rest of Us

Most people like to read and listen to accounts of the accomplishments of successful leaders and entrepreneurs; about their vision, commitment, and ability to inspire and motivate others toward the achievement of great business successes, Super Bowl victories, and scientific breakthroughs.

Hearing about the characteristics of successful business leaders and team leaders is enjoyable. Even though we have heard it many times before, and always agree with everything that is said, it inspires us and makes us feel good. We almost always conclude that we also possess many of their characteristics and abilities.

But telling a banker that he or she must become a visionary, an entrepreneur, a motivator, a strategist, and a communicator to be an effective manager is much like a basketball coach telling a room full of athletes that he wants someone with speed, quickness, good hands, and the ability to see the whole floor to be the point guard that will lead the team to victory.

Both instances involve information that is certainly valid, practical, realistic, hardheaded, down-to-earth advice. You certainly cannot disagree with any of it. But in both cases the information isn't very useful.

Everyone talks about good leadership being important, but little is done about it. Saying the word over and over again— *leadership, leadership, leadership,* won't do us much good. Good intentions will only take us so far. What we need to know is *how* to do these things and what the barriers to implementation are.

The aspiring basketball point guard should be asking "How do I know if I have speed, quickness, good hands, and the ability to see the whole floor, and if I don't, how do I get them?" Bankers desiring to improve their management and leadership skills should be asking the same questions about vision, strategic thinking, and motivation and leadership skills. Being told what we need to do and be is one thing. Becoming it is another thing entirely. There is nothing wrong with inspiration and we can all use some of it. But it's a long road from inspiration to implementation, and it is time to begin the journey.

---

Developing competent bankers who are also effective managers and leaders is one of the critical human resource challenges facing the banking industry.

---

## THE CHALLENGE TO THE BANKER

There is little doubt that the demand for bankers who can also manage will increase during the next decade. In fact, the demand in the industry for managerial talent will exceed the supply.

How does a banker who really wants to improve his or her management or leadership skills begin? An individual who would really want to do more than be inpsired by reading or hearing about what good managers and leaders do and have, and who has decided to take greater personal responsibility for career planning and management should begin this personal assessment with these two questions:

1. Do I want to manage?
2. Can I manage?

## The Will to Manage (Do I Want to Manage?)

The critical questions here are, "Do I have the desire or need to influence the performance of others?" and "Do I derive satisfaction from doing so?" This desire has been termed the "will to manage."[5] Psychologists who have studied the will to manage have found it related to several important attitudes:[6]

- A favorable attitude toward authority.
- A need to compete.
- A need to be assertive.
- A need to exercise power.
- A need to stand out in a group.
- A sense of responsibility.

The greater the strength of these attitudes, the more likely an individual is to select management as a career and the more likely they are to achieve success. Very importantly, the will to manage can be strengthened through training.[7]

In his wonderful book *The Empowered Manager*, Peter Block discusses three personal choices that managers make that shape their work environment.[8] We find his ideas to be particularly useful for bankers assessing their individual will to manage, as well as extremely descriptive of the management needs of the industry itself. According to Block, a manager makes three fundamental choices:

- A choice between maintenance and greatness.
- A choice between caution and courage.
- A choice between dependency and autonomy.

*Maintenance versus Greatness.* Managers choosing maintenance try to hold on to what they themselves have created or inherited from a previous manager. Their goal is not to lose any ground. Block notes that a bureaucratic culture drives managers toward a maintenance mentality. The bureaucratic belief is that we move ahead in the organization by not making mistakes. Accordingly, we surround ourselves with an insulation of structure and predictability.

The alternative choice is greatness. The personal choice for greatness is the commitment to operate and achieve in a unique way. Choosing a unique path in a bureaucracy is risky and dangerous and therefore, signifies an entrepreneurial spirit. Block believes that each of us has the opportunity to make a commitment to greatness in our own managerial job.

*Caution versus Courage.*   Bank managers receive many organizational signals to be careful and cautious. For example, performance reviews and presentations to management are just two of many events that symbolize the pressure to be careful, to not make a mistake.

But taking a bank or a unit of a bank and moving it forward involves courage. Courage is a different path than caution and is often an unpopular path. Block notes that courage in an organization is different from courage in other situations where an issue is good or bad, or clearly defined. Courage in an organization is required when the sides are somewhat murky, when the issue may not be a big one, and when top management is not on your side.

*Dependency versus Autonomy.*   Block believes that autonomy is the attitude that our actions are our own choices and the organization we are a part of is in many ways our own creation. This kind of attitude puts us in the center and in charge of what is happening at the moment. However, he notes that it is difficult to maintain an attitude of autonomy in a hierarchy of many levels. Such an environment feeds the feeling of dependency.

We hear a consistent cry for strong leadership in banking. Over and over again we hear that "We can do nothing without top management support." Perhaps the most popular reason for their failures according to bank managers is a lack of support of their efforts by top management. Top management is blamed for not having vision, and not providing direction, leadership, and motivation.

According to Block, all of these wishes for changes above us are an expression of dependency. They imply that until something above us changes, we can do little to improve our own performance. Constantly looking upward for guidance and direction is an expression of our dependency.

However, when we choose autonomy, he states that:

> We realize that there is nothing to wait for. We do not require anything from those above us to create a unit or department of our own choosing. An autonomous or entrepreneurial mind-set means that I must commit myself to managing my unit in a way that makes sense to me and that the weight of the organization is on my shoulders.[9]

Incidentially, deciding that the future of our unit is in our own hands, is according to Block, also good for the organization as a whole.

In our opinion, Block's three choices are timely ones for bank managers to consider. The three choices focus us down an entrepreneurial path, a critical one for bankers to assess at this state of our industry's evolution.

In conclusion, assessing your will to manage means answering the question, "Do I want to manage?" If your answer is yes, the industry sorely needs you to also choose greatness, courage, and autonomy.

---

It is a long road from inspiration to implementation.

---

### Assessing Your Potential to Be a Manager (Can I Manage?)

A banker who has the will to manage would be wise to also determine if he or she has the ability to manage. It is now possible, with the assistance of career counseling professionals, to determine our potential as a manager and leader.

Thus, the challenge to the individual banker considering a move to management is to confront the issues: *Do I have the will to manage and do I have or can I develop the ability to man-*

*age?* Confronting these two issues is the first step in career planning.

Where should the individual banker begin? There are literally thousands of ideas, programs, concepts, books, methods, and audio and video programs that are excellent means of self-development for bankers wanting to improve their effectiveness as a manager and a leader.

However, before you decide to transform your leadership style, sign up for a survival camp, or walk over hot coals, there are some questions you may want to ask. They can also be useful before you sign up for less ambitious pursuits such as schools, short courses, and seminars. There are surely other questions but these will get you started.

**1.** *Does it provide a quick fix?* There is no fun and easy way to become an effective manager and leader. Many such ways are available and the fact that many of them outsell the works of Peter Drucker is testimony to the preference for the fun and easy over the hard and difficult. But a real commitment to professional and self-development usually occurs after the quick fix has been rejected.

**2.** *What will it do for me?* Can you define the benefit in one sentence? The benefit must be clear and it must be definable. And, whatever it is supposed to do, it should do it more than once. In other words, the benefit should be renewable and repeatable—you should receive it more than once. If all you get is one good jolt of the "feel goods," then what you are probably getting is inspiration. But as we said earlier, bankers serious about becoming effective managers and leaders must move beyond inspiration.

**3.** *Can I teach it to others?* You should be able to teach it to someone in your bank and/or modify it to suit your bank or department. For example, a simple time management course will usually offer benefits that are renewable and repeatable (you can use what you have learned every day), and you can teach the principles to others.

**4.** *Can I measure results?* Will you be a more effective planner, communicator, supervisor, trainer, coach, and/or time manager? Will it improve your thinking? Will it produce measurable results?

## THE CHALLENGE TO THE BANK

Determining whether one has the will to manage and the potential to manage is the responsibility of the individual banker. They are also the first two steps in career planning. At that point, career planning for managers becomes the responsibility of the bank. This is because recognizing their need for managerial talent and taking the steps to ensure that the talent is developed and ready when needed, is the responsibility of the bank.

Although still a relatively new practice, many banks are turning to career planning as a way to *proact* rather than *react* to problems associated with developing much needed managerial talent. The alternative is to continue to do it as it was done in the past, rewarding those who have been successful in a technical banking specialty with a management position. *Career planning* involves matching an individual's career aspirations with the opportunities available in the bank. *Career pathing* is the sequencing of specific jobs associated with those opportunities.

The career planning and pathing process is described in Figure 8–2. The important point to note is that it places equal responsibility on the individual and the bank.[10] Individuals must identify their aspirations and abilities and, through counseling, recognize the training and development required for a particular career path. The bank must identify their managerial needs and opportunities and, through human resource planning, provide the training and development to their employees. Career planning cannot proceed from either the individual or bank point of view unless career paths and requirements have been identified and the information made available. If implemented effectively, career planning can satisfy the needs of both the individual and the bank.

## THE CHALLENGE TO THE INDUSTRY

One of the most important lessons we learned while writing this book is that the set of skills required to be an effective

**FIGURE 8-2**
**The Challenge to the Bank: Career Planning**

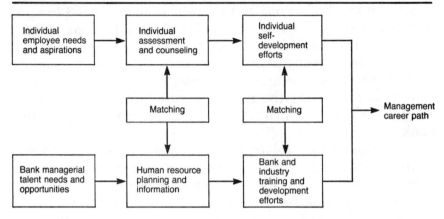

manager in a bank has not only enlarged, but the mix of the three skills in the set has also shifted. Greater and more sophisticated technical banking skills are required. However, certain conceptual skills and human skills not required in the past are today as important as technical banking skills. In fact, it is a consensus among the bankers we spoke with that conceptual and human skills will provide the competitive edge in the future.

Individual bankers and banks will, in the future, look to those organizations that they have looked to in the past to provide for the educational and training needs of the industry. These organizations have educated generations of bankers in the technical skills and functional specialties of the industry. Continued excellence in technical education will be no small challenge.

The real challenge, however, will be the development of the human and conceptual skills required to be an effective manager and leader in the new world of banking. Thus, developing the new banker will mean developing bankers who can also manage an organization as well as people. To do any less will be to develop pools of inadequate human resources.

During the five years of research for this book, we developed some strong beliefs about what specific human and conceptual skills bankers need and want. Our suggested program consists of two components. The first component focuses on the human skills necessary for bank management. The second component focuses on conceptual skills. Some of the subject matter is not found in most industry educational programs.[11]

---

Successful managers and leaders are like the rest of us: a patchwork of strengths and weaknesses.

---

## Human Skills

Five skills comprise this component:

**1.** *Confronting the role of manager-leader.* We found a reluctance among many bankers to accept the importance of developing their human skills. This reluctance is no doubt a consequence of previous experiences which conditioned many existing bank managers to believe that they alone can do the work of the bank and that the employees' contributions are marginal. We know from this book that the changing banking work force will require future managers to understand the demands of their jobs and the role of a manager-leader. They will be forced to gauge realistically the match between the demands of the job and their own will to manage, and ability to manage.

**2.** *Communication skills.* Bank managers communicate ideas to numerous groups in a variety of settings. The primary medium is oral rather than written and the primary message is the underlying concept of the bank and its strategy. Effectively communicating a vision and a strategy requires the ability to communicate persuasively as well as to inform.

**3.** *Team-building skills.* Our research clearly indicates that bank managers do much of their work in group settings, including management teams, task forces, problem-solving sessions, commissions, and committees. In these situations the quality of work depends not only on the skills of the individual members, but also on their ability to work as a team.

**4.** *Decision-making skills.* Bank managers usually make decisions based on staff work. The staff identifies issues, gathers information, presents alternatives, and recommends action. The manager decides to reject or accept the staff's decision, rather than make a decision about the issue itself. Even in the smallest of community banks, managers must often decide among alternative decisions that employees propose. The distinction between approving the decisions of others and making a decision is an important one in understanding the changing management job in banking. And the skills required in these situations differ from those required prior to deregulation.

5. *Leadership skills.* A bank manager leads an organization or part of an organization as well as people. Through the use of ideas, rituals, and symbols, leaders build support and acceptance of their vision and strategy. Effective leadership is the result of the application of communication, team building, and decision-making skills. Its effective implementation requires integration of these skills into a consistent and coherent pattern of behavior.

## Conceptual Skills

Five skills comprise this component:

1. *Environmental analysis skills.* A distinguishing feature of how the new banker will spend his or her time is the prominence of the external environment. They must continually match the strategies of their bank or unit with the opportunities and threats of the environment. The required skills include being able to identify relevant environmental forces, sensing the strength and direction of these forces, acquiring pertinent information, and interpreting trends and cycles.

2. *Strategic analysis skills.* It is difficult to find a banker who does not acknowledge the importance of strategic analysis and planning as the process by which the bank's mission and objectives are infused throughout the organization. The process takes the information obtained by environmental analysis, confronts it with an assessment of the bank's capabilities, and selects alternative strategies to pursue.

3. *Organization design skills.* We already know from Chapters 6 and 7 that organizations must be designed to implement strategy. This idea differs greatly from the prede-

regulation idea of organization structure as an instrument of control. Effective bank managers understand the impact of organization structure on performance.

**4.** *Interorganizational analysis skills.* Banks interact with other banks and organizations and the substance of that interaction is a large part of the world the new banker must understand. It will become increasingly important as merger activities and continued deregulation demand skill in competition and coalition, joint venturing, bargaining and negotiation, and cooperation.

**5.** *Change management skills.* Managers and leaders create and manage organizations. They also in one way or another, change and develop them. We have seen throughout this book that skill in effectively managing change is critical for all bank managers.

These 10 skills present an integrated constellation of what we believe are much needed human and conceptual skills. The challenge to the banking industry is to provide those individuals who are technically skilled in banking, have the will to manage, and have the ability to manage with the opportunity to develop the critical human and conceptual skills which our research has found to be related to effective bank management.

# NOTES

## Chapter 1

1. Arthur Andersen & Co., *The Decade of Change: Banking in Europe—The Next Ten Years* (London: Lafferty Publications, Ltd., 1986) and Association of Reserve City Banks and Arthur Andersen & Co., *Strategic Issues in Banking* (Chicago: Arthur Andersen and Co., 1985).
2. Robert L. Katz, "Skills of an Effective Administrator," *Harvard Business Review*, September–October 1974. Katz is one of the earliest writers to discuss the three skills outlined here.

## Chapter 2

1. Daniel Yankelovich and Associates, *Work and Human Values* (New York: Public Agenda Foundation, 1983), pp. 6–7.
2. The concept of discretionary effort was developed by Daniel Yankelovich and John Immerwahr in their *Putting the Work Ethic to Work* (New York: Public Agenda Foundation, 1983), p. 1. Their concept was the catalyst for all of our ideas on peak performance in banking.
3. James H. Donnelly, Jr., Leonard L. Berry, and Thomas W. Thompson, *Marketing Financial Services: A Strategic Vision* (Homewood, Ill.: Dow Jones-Irwin, 1985), chapter 12.
4. The discussion of the low- and high-discretion workplace models is adapted from Yankelovich and Immerwahr, *Putting the Work Ethic to Work*, pp. 1–18. The application to banking is ours.
5. Summarized from Yankelovich and Immerwahr, pp. 11–18.
6. Ibid., p. 23.
7. Ibid., p. 7.
8. Ibid.
9. Adapted from James H. Donnelly, Jr., "Workaday Encounters Provide Six Service Lessons," *American Banker*, August 11, 1988, p. 4.

## Chapter 3

1. From James H. Donnelly, Jr., "Vision of Greatness Can Be a Powerful Motivator," *American Banker*, November 17, 1988, p. 4.
2. John Naisbett, *Megatrends: Ten New Directions Transforming Our Lives* (New York: Warner Books, 1984), chapter 5.
3. Peter Block, *The Empowered Manager* (San Francisco: Jossey-Bass, 1988), pp. 121–22.
4. From James H. Donnelly, Jr., "Bankers Could Learn a Lesson from Doctors," *American Banker*, March 17, 1988, p. 4.
5. This discussion is based on the work of Thomas V. Bonoma, *The Marketing Edge: Making Strategies Work* (New York: Free Press, 1985), pp. 12–14.
6. Based on Benjamin B. Tregoe and John W. Zimmerman, *Top Management Strategy: What It Is and How to Make It Work* (New York: Simon & Schuster, 1980), pp. 34–37.

## Chapter 4

1. Adapted from an earlier work, James L. Gibson and James H. Donnelly, Jr., "A Banker's Guide to Managing Change through Organizational Development," *Journal of Retail Banking*, Summer 1987, pp. 5–15.
2. James L. Gibson, John M. Ivancevich, and James H. Donnelly, Jr., *Organizations: Behavior, Structure, Processes*, 6th ed. (Plano, Tex.: Business Publications, 1988), p. 695.
3. Our strategy puts into practice some of the ideas of organizational development. Organizational development is a management technique directed at improving individual, group and organizational effectiveness through the application of relevant behavioral science knowledge.
4. See Larry E. Greiner, "Patterns of Organizational Change," *Harvard Business Review*, May–June 1967, pp. 119–30.
5. Gibson, Ivancevich, and Donnelly, chapter 19.
6. Gibson, Ivancevich, and Donnelly, p. 722.

## Chapter 5

1. Larry E. Greiner, "Patterns of Organization Change," *Harvard Business Review*, May–June 1967, p. 119.
2. Adapted from James L. Gibson, John M. Ivancevich, and James

H. Donnelly, Jr., *Organizations: Behavior, Structure, Processes*, 6th ed. (Plano, Tex.: Business Publications, 1988), p. 724.
3. Adapted from James H. Donnelly, Jr., James L. Gibson, and John M. Ivancevich, *Fundamentals of Management*, 6th ed. (Plano, Tex.: Business Publications, 1987), p. 480.
4. James L. Gibson and James H. Donnelly, Jr., "A Banker's Guide to Managing Change through Organizational Development," *Journal of Retail Banking*, Summer 1987, p. 14.
5. Four reasons are discussed in John P. Kotter and Leonard A. Schlesinger, "Choosing Strategies for Change," *Harvard Business Review*, March–April 1979, pp. 106–14.
6. Kotter and Schlesinger, p. 112.

## Chapter 6

1. Adapted from James H. Donnelly, Jr., "Bank Organizational Structures: An Editorial Viewpoint," *Journal of Retail Banking*, Fall 1985, pp. 11–12.
2. James L. Gibson, John M. Ivancevich, and James H. Donnelly, Jr., *Organizations: Behavior, Structure, Processes*, 6th ed. (Plano, Tex.: Business Publications, 1988), chapter 12.
3. See Gibson, Ivancevich, and Donnelly, chapter 12, for a detailed discussion of the key concepts of organizational design.
4. Tom Peters, *Thriving on Chaos* (New York: Alfred A. Knopf, 1987), p. 467.
5. Adapted from an earlier work, James L. Gibson and James H. Donnelly, Jr., "Integrating Strategy and Structure: Achieving a Market-Oriented Financial Institution," *Journal of Retail Banking*, Fall 1985, pp. 13–23.

## Chapter 7

1. Some material in this chapter was drawn from two previous works: James H. Donnelly, Jr., Leonard L. Berry, and Thomas W. Thompson, *Marketing Financial Services: A Strategic Vision* (Homewood, Ill.: Dow Jones-Irwin, 1985), chapter 4; and James L. Gibson and James H. Donnelly, Jr., "Integrating Organizational Structure and Strategy: Achieving a Market-Oriented Financial Institution," *Journal of Retail Banking*, Fall 1985, pp. 13–23.
2. Thomas W. Thompson, Leonard L. Berry, and James H. Donnelly, Jr., "The Marketing/Retail Banking Partnership: An Evo-

lutionary Perspective," *Journal of Retail Banking*, Summer 1985, pp. 9–22.

3. Alena Wells, "How Citicorp Restructured for the Eighties," *Euromoney*, April 1980, pp. 13–24.

## Chapter 8

1. Summarized from Bernard M. Bass, *Stogdill's Handbook of Leadership* (New York: Free Press, 1982), pp. 75–76.
2. Bernard M. Bass, *Leadership and Performance Beyond Expectations* (New York: Free Press, 1985).
3. R. J. House, "A 1976 Theory of Charismatic Leadership," in *Leadership: The Cutting Edge*, ed. J. G. Hunt and L. L. Larson (Carbondale: Southern Illinois University Press, 1977), pp. 105–207.
4. Reported in Morgan W. McCall, Jr., and Michael W. Lombardo, "What Makes a Top Executive?" *Psychology Today*, February 1983, pp. 26–31.
5. Sterling Livingston, "Myth of the Well-Educated Manager," *Harvard Business Review*, January–February 1971, pp. 79–89; John B. Miner, *The Challenge of Managing* (Philadelphia: W. B. Saunders, 1975), p. 276.
6. Miner, ibid., pp. 220–23.
7. Ibid., p. 296.
8. Peter Block, *The Empowered Manager: Positive Political Skills at Work* (San Francisco: Jossey-Bass, 1987), pp. 7–17.
9. Ibid., pp. 16–17.
10. James H. Donnelly, Jr., James L. Gibson, and John M. Ivancevich, *Fundamentals of Management*, 6th ed. (Plano, Tex.: Business Publications, 1987), p. 715.
11. James H. Donnelly, Jr., James L. Gibson, and Steven J. Skinner, "The Behaviors of Effective Bank Managers," *Journal of Retail Banking*, Winter 1988, pp. 29–37.

# INDEX